# Reid's Read-Alouds

**Other Booklist Publications**

*The Back Page,* by Bill Ott

# Reid's Read-Alouds

Selections for Children and Teens

## Rob Reid

American Library Association
Chicago   2009

**Rob Reid** is the very popular author of numerous books on children's programming for ALA Editions. He has also written resource books for Upstart Books, as well as two picture books. In addition, he writes regular columns on programming and children's literature for *LibrarySparks* and *Book Links* magazines. He teaches courses on children's and adolescent literature and a variety of library topics at the University of Wisconsin–Eau Claire. He conducts workshops throughout North America on ways to make literature come alive for children.

The paper used in this publication meets the minimum requirements of American National Standard for Information Sciences—Permanence of Paper for Printed Library Materials, ANSI Z39.48-1992. ∞

Library of Congress Cataloging-in-Publication Data
Reid, Rob.
  Reid's read-alouds : selections for children and teens / Rob Reid.
     p.   cm.
  Includes bibliographical references.
     ISBN 978-0-8389-0980-5 (alk. paper)
  1. Children—Books and reading—United States. 2. Children's literature—Bibliography.
3. Young adult literature—Bibliography. 4. Oral reading. 5. School libraries—Activity programs—United States. I. Title.
Z1037.R54 2009
011.62—dc22                                                                          2008045376

ISBN-13: 978-0-8389-0980-5

Printed in the United States of America
13 12 11 10 09        5 4 3 2 1

To Parker

# Contents

# Acknowledgments

I'd like to thank the following:

Laura Tillotson, for inviting me to join the *Book Links* family

everyone through the years at ALA Editions

Eloise Kinney and her sharp eyes

Jim Trelease, author of *The Read-Aloud Handbook,* for his inspiration

the circulation staff and the Interlibrary Loan Department at the L. E. Phillips Memorial Public Library for having my stack of books ready for me as I walk in the building

Vicki and Steve Palmquist and my other friends at the Children's Literature Network

the children's and young adult authors who wrote such marvelous books— keep them coming

my students at the University of Wisconsin–Eau Claire

my family

and the children and teens who listened and responded

Many of the annotations in this book appeared in similar form in my articles for *Book Links* magazine and appear here with the kind permission of the magazine's publisher.

# Introduction

I love to read. With my name, how could I not? I read as a child, as a teen, and as an adult. I read aloud to my children when they were younger, and I read to thousands of other people's children in public library and school settings. I continue today to read to children in various settings and to my university students, who will become tomorrow's teachers, librarians, and parents.

This book really began a few years ago, when Laura Tillotson, editor of *Book Links* magazine, invited me to write an article about the funniest children's classics for their fifteenth-anniversary issue. I was flattered by the invitation and wrote that article as well as a companion article on contemporary children's humor books. That second article contained a feature I call the "10-Minute Selection," a short read-aloud passage from a book that can entertain children and teens as a stand-alone piece. These selections are in reality anywhere between five and fifteen minutes. I would read such passages as a public children's librarian for visiting groups. Many kids would inevitably request that particular book so they could read it in its entirety. I didn't worry about the kids who weren't interested in doing follow-up reading. I figured we just spent some entertaining, quality literature time together, and perhaps I could interest them in another book.

Back to *Book Links*. I wrote more articles on great read-alouds for young people. Each article highlighted several books on a particular topic, and each annotation contained a "10-Minute Selection." Both *Book Links* and I received positive responses from the magazine's audience. Again, I was flattered in late 2007 when Laura offered me my own *Book Links* column, titled "The Reid-Aloud Alert," which began in early 2008. *Reid's Read-Alouds: Selections for Children and Teens* builds on that column.

For every book in this collection, I read another handful that I chose not to include because of many factors. Those books may have more personal or delicate content that's not as conducive to a mixed group of kids as it is to an individual reader. The language may be too strong, which could lead to an uncomfortable group situation.

The books that *were* chosen for this collection are a mixture of strong read-alouds aimed at readers from elementary school through high school. I looked for variety and a balance of genres, topics, and perspectives, particularly in regard to gender. Some of the books are award winners, and some will cause literary critics to roll their eyes. They all appeal to young listeners, however. Most of these books demonstrate strong writing with a flowing text that is a delight to read aloud. The books chosen need to be long enough to take more than one sitting to read. That's why there are fewer titles for children in primary elementary school (grades K–2) than for older kids and teens. I also chose children's and young adult books published between 2000 and 2008 to provide more focus for this project. There are hundreds of great read-aloud titles published before 2000 that I will revisit and highlight in the future. The 200 titles chosen here are just a small representation of great read-aloud books currently on the market. I hope to continue locating more of them—older and newer titles—for upcoming *Book Links* articles.

## REID'S READ-ALOUD TIPS

Know your audience. They may prefer a specific type of book. Some audiences may not be able to handle scary books, while another audience may clamor for more. I have included general age recommendations for each book, but don't be limited by them. Many younger groups can easily handle titles recommended for slightly older groups. One reason I list all of the titles in this collection together regardless of age level is because I don't want to completely pigeonhole books in one age category or another. I would not hesitate to read Kate DiCamillo's book *The Tale of Despereaux* to certain kindergartners even though the book is listed here as recommended for children in grades 2–5. Other groups of kindergarteners, on the other hand, may not be able to handle the book. Know your audience.

Challenge your audience. Share a book that some kids may not normally choose on their own. Two great examples are Shannon Hale's books *The Goose Girl* and *Princess Academy*. The latter title was my favorite fantasy of 2005, the year I served on the Newbery Award Committee. I knew boys would love both titles but wouldn't necessarily pick them up on their own because of the titles and jackets. Once the stories started, however, I found that both girls and boys were captivated by the exploits of Hale's lively, strong characters. Challenge older audiences to listen to younger material they may have missed when they were younger. There's no reason not to read a book such as *Elijah of Buxton,* by

Christopher Paul Curtis, to high schoolers, even though the book isn't marketed to this age group. Challenge your audience.

Entertain your audience. Choose books you yourself have read and enjoyed. Your enthusiasm will carry over into your reading. Be prepared so you can handle vocabulary, names, and foreign phrases that are new to you. Don't read a book you haven't read in advance. Project your voice. Make sure the person in the back can hear your every word, even during the quiet, serious passages. Add variety to your vocalization. Trust the author's words. Entertain your audience.

Even though I hope you don't limit yourself to the age levels given for each title if you know your audience can handle it, I have included lists in the back matter that group titles by the following grade levels: early elementary (K–2), upper elementary (3–5), middle school (6–8), and high school (9–12). I have also included a subject listing.

Finally, I can't say enough about the influence of Jim Trelease on thousands of readers over the years. I have always maintained that his *Read-Aloud Handbook* was—and continues to be—the most important book found in any library I have worked in or used as a patron. I saw Jim speak to a large group of teachers back in 1986, early in my career as a librarian. He reaffirmed my career decision for me, and I'm forever grateful that he stepped forward to promote literacy.

# Authors and Titles at a Glance

Abrams, Peter. *Down the Rabbit Hole*. HarperCollins, 2005.
Anderson, Laurie Halse. *Fever 1793*. Simon and Schuster, 2000.
Archer, Lily. *The Poison Apples*. Feiwel and Friends, 2007.
Armstrong, Alan. *Whittington*. Random House, 2005.
Auch, Mary Jane. *I Was a Third Grade Spy*. Holiday House, 2001.
Avi. *Ereth's Birthday*. HarperCollins, 2000.
———. *The Secret School*. Harcourt, 2001.
———. *The Traitor's Gate*. Atheneum, 2007.
Barrows, Annie. *Ivy and Bean and the Ghost That Had to Go*. Chronicle, 2006.
Bauer, Joan. *Hope Was Here*. Putnam, 2000.
———. *Peeled*. Putnam, 2008.
Bauer, Marion Dane. *The Double-Digit Club*. Holiday House, 2004.
Birdsall, Jeanne. *The Penderwicks: A Summer Tale of Four Sisters, Two Rabbits,
    and a Very Interesting Boy*. Knopf, 2005.
Birney, Betty G. *The Seven Wonders of Sassafras Springs*. Atheneum, 2005.
Bledsoe, Lucy Jane. *Hoop Girlz*. Holiday House, 2002.
Blume, Judy. *Soupy Saturdays with the Pain and the Great One*. Delacorte, 2007.
Bowe, Julie. *My Last Best Friend*. Harcourt, 2007.
Bowler, Tim. *Storm Catchers*. Margaret K. McElderry, 2001.
Broach, Elise. *Shakespeare's Secret*. Holt, 2005.
Bruchac, Joseph. *Bearwalker*. HarperCollins, 2007.
———. *The Dark Pond*. HarperCollins, 2004.
Buckley, Michael. *The Sisters Grimm, Book One: The Fairy Tale Detectives*.
    Amulet, 2005.
Byars, Betsy. *Keeper of the Doves*. Viking, 2002.
———. *Me Tarzan*. HarperCollins, 2000.
Byars, Betsy, Betsy Duffey, and Laurie Myers. *The SOS File*. Holt, 2004.
Cabot, Meg. *Jinx*. HarperCollins, 2007.

Cameron, Ann. *Gloria's Way.* Farrar Straus Giroux, 2000.

Carter, Alden. *Love, Football, and Other Contact Sports.* Holiday House, 2006.

Clements, Andrew. *Jake Drake, Class Clown.* Simon and Schuster, 2002.

———. *No Talking.* Simon and Schuster, 2007.

———. *A Week in the Woods.* Simon and Schuster, 2002.

Colfer, Eoin. *Artemis Fowl.* Hyperion, 2001.

———. *The Supernaturalist.* Hyperion, 2004.

Collins, Ross. *Medusa Jones.* Scholastic, 2008.

Coombs, Kate. *The Runaway Princess.* Farrar Straus Giroux, 2006.

Craig, Joe. *Jimmy Coates: Assassin?* HarperCollins, 2005.

Creech, Sharon. *Granny Torrelli Makes Soup.* Joanna Cotler, 2003.

———. *Heartbeat.* HarperCollins, 2004.

———. *The Wanderer.* HarperCollins, 2000.

Cummings, Priscilla. *Red Kayak.* Dutton, 2004.

Curtis, Christopher Paul. *Elijah of Buxton.* Scholastic, 2007.

———. *Mr. Chickee's Funny Money.* Wendy Lamb, 2005.

Cushman, Karen. *Matilda Bone.* Clarion, 2000.

———. *Rodzina.* Clarion, 2003.

Cutler, Jane. *Leap, Frog.* Farrar Straus Giroux, 2002.

Delaney, Joseph. *The Last Apprentice: Revenge of the Witch.* Greenwillow, 2005.

Delaney, Michael. *Birdbrain Amos.* Philomel, 2002.

Denslow, Sharon Phillips. *Georgie Lee.* Greenwillow, 2002.

DiCamillo, Kate. *Because of Winn-Dixie.* Candlewick, 2000.

———. *The Miraculous Journey of Edward Tulane.* Candlewick, 2006.

———. *The Tale of Despereaux.* Candlewick, 2003.

Dowd, Siobhan. *The London Eye Mystery.* David Fickling, 2007.

Dowell, Frances O'Roark. *Dovey Coe.* Atheneum, 2000.

———. *Phineas L. MacGuire . . . Erupts! The First Experiment.* Atheneum, 2006.

Draper, Sharon M. *Double Dutch.* Atheneum, 2002.

Dunrea, Olivier. *Hanne's Quest.* Philomel, 2006.

DuPrau, Jeanne. *Car Trouble.* Greenwillow, 2005.

———. *The City of Ember.* Random House, 2003.

Dyer, Heather. *Ibby's Magic Weekend.* Scholastic, 2008.

Elliott, David. *Evangeline Mudd and the Golden-Haired Apes of the Ikkinasti Jungle.* Candlewick, 2004.

Erdrich, Louise. *The Game of Silence.* HarperCollins, 2005.

Fama, Elizabeth. *Overboard.* Cricket, 2002.

Fine, Anne. *The Jamie and Angus Stories.* Candlewick, 2002.

Flake, Sharon B. *Begging for Change.* Hyperion, 2003.

Funke, Cornelia. *Igraine the Brave.* Scholastic, 2007.

———. *Inkheart.* Scholastic, 2003.

Gaiman, Neil. *Coraline.* HarperCollins, 2002.

Gallo, Donald R., ed. *Destination Unexpected.* Candlewick, 2003.

———, ed. *First Crossing: Stories about Teen Immigrants.* Candlewick, 2004.

Gantos, Jack. *Jack Adrift: Fourth Grade without a Clue.* Farrar Straus Giroux, 2003.

Gardner, Lyn. *Into the Woods.* David Fickling, 2006.

Giff, Patricia Reilly. *Willow Run.* Wendy Lamb, 2005.

Glatshteyn, Yankev. *Emil and Karl.* Roaring Brook, 2006.

Graff, Nancy Price. *Taking Wing.* Clarion, 2005.

Grant, Michael. *Gone.* HarperCollins, 2008.

Griffin, Adele. *My Almost Epic Summer.* Putnam, 2006.

Grimes, Nikki. *Bronx Masquerade.* Dial, 2002.

Haddix, Margaret Peterson. *Found.* Simon and Schuster, 2008.

———. *Say What?* Simon and Schuster, 2004.

Hale, Bruce. *The Possum Always Rings Twice.* Harcourt, 2006.

Hale, Shannon. *The Goose Girl.* Bloomsbury, 2003.

———. *Princess Academy.* Bloomsbury, 2005.

Harkrader, L. D. *Airball: My Life in Briefs.* Roaring Brook, 2005.

Hautman, Peter. *Rash.* Simon and Schuster, 2006.

Hautman, Peter, and Mary Logue. *Snatched.* Putnam, 2006.

Heneghan, James. *Payback.* Groundwood, 2007.

Hiaasen, Carl. *Flush.* Knopf, 2005.

———. *Hoot.* Knopf, 2002.

Higgins, F. E. *The Black Book of Secrets.* Feiwel and Friends, 2007.

Hill, Kirkpatrick. *The Year of Miss Agnes.* Margaret K. McElderry, 2000.

Hobbs, Will. *Wild Man Island.* HarperCollins, 2002.

Horvath, Polly. *The Pepins and Their Problems.* Farrar Straus Giroux, 2004.

Hunter, Erin. *Warriors: Into the Wild.* HarperCollins, 2003.

Jenkins, Emily. *Toys Go Out.* Schwartz and Wade, 2006.

Johnson, Angela. *Bird.* Dial, 2004.

Jonell, Lynne. *Emmy and the Incredible Shrinking Rat.* Holt, 2007.

Kerrin, Jessica Scott. *Martin Bridge: Ready for Takeoff!* Kids Can, 2005.

Key, Watt. *Alabama Moon.* Farrar Straus Giroux, 2006.

King-Smith, Dick. *Lady Lollipop.* Candlewick, 2000.

Korman, Gordon. *Island: Book One; Shipwreck.* Scholastic, 2001.

———. *No More Dead Dogs.* Hyperion, 2000.

Landy, Derek. *Skulduggery Pleasant.* HarperCollins, 2007.

Larson, Kirby. *Hattie Big Sky.* Delacorte, 2006.

Look, Lenore. *Alvin Ho: Allergic to Girls, School, and Other Scary Things.* Schwartz and Wade, 2008.

———. *Ruby Lu, Empress of Everything.* Atheneum, 2006.

Lord, Cynthia. *Rules.* Scholastic, 2006.
Lorey, Dean. *Nightmare Academy.* HarperCollins, 2007.
Lowry, Lois. *Gathering Blue.* Houghton Mifflin, 2000.
———. *Gooney Bird Greene.* Houghton Mifflin, 2002.
Lupica, Mike. *Heat.* Philomel, 2006.
Mackel, Kathy. *MadCat.* HarperCollins, 2005.
Maguire, Gregory. *Leaping Beauty and Other Animal Fairy Tales.* HarperCollins, 2004.
———. *Three Rotten Eggs.* Clarion, 2002.
Marcantonio, Patricia Santos. *Red Ridin' in the Hood and Other Cuentos.* Farrar Straus Giroux, 2005.
Marsden, Carolyn. *Moon Runner.* Candlewick, 2005.
McCaughrean, Geraldine. *Cyrano.* Harcourt, 2006.
———. *The Kite Rider.* HarperCollins, 2001.
McDonald, Megan. *Judy Moody.* Candlewick, 2000.
———. *Stink and the Incredible Super-Galactic Jawbreaker.* Candlewick, 2006.
Mercado, Nancy E., ed. *Tripping Over the Lunch Lady and Other School Stories.* Dial, 2004.
Michael, Livi. *City of Dogs.* Putnam, 2007.
Miller, Sarah. *Miss Spitfire: Reaching Helen Keller.* Atheneum, 2007.
Morgenstern, Susie. *A Book of Coupons.* Viking, 2001.
Morpurgo, Michael. *Private Peaceful.* Scholastic, 2003.
Morris, Gerald. *The Adventures of Sir Lancelot the Great.* Houghton Mifflin, 2008.
———. *The Lioness and Her Knight.* Houghton Mifflin, 2005.
Murdock, Catherine Gilbert. *Dairy Queen.* Houghton Mifflin, 2006.
Myers, Walter Dean. *Harlem Summer.* Scholastic, 2007.
———. *Sunrise over Fallujah.* Scholastic, 2008.
Nagdo, Ann Whitehead. *Tarantula Power.* Holiday House, 2007.
Naidoo, Beverley. *The Other Side of Truth.* HarperCollins, 2000.
Napoli, Donna Jo, and Robert Furrow. *Sly the Sleuth and the Sports Mysteries.* Dial, 2006.
Naylor, Phyllis Reynolds. *Polo's Mother.* Atheneum, 2005.
———. *Roxie and the Hooligans.* Atheneum, 2006.
O'Connor, Barbara. *How to Steal a Dog.* Farrar Straus Giroux, 2007.
Park, Linda Sue. *Archer's Quest.* Clarion, 2006.
———. *Project Mulberry.* Clarion, 2005.
Paterson, Katherine. *The Same Stuff as Stars.* Clarion, 2002.
Paulsen, Gary. *Brian's Hunt.* Wendy Lamb, 2003.
———. *How Angel Peterson Got His Name and Other Outrageous Tales about Extreme Sports.* Wendy Lamb, 2003.

Pearsall, Shelley. *All Shook Up.* Knopf, 2008.

Peck, Richard. *On the Wings of Heroes.* Dial, 2007.

————. *Past Perfect, Present Tense: New and Collected Stories.* Dial, 2004.

————. *The Teacher's Funeral: A Comedy in Three Parts.* Dial, 2004.

Pennypacker, Sara. *The Talented Clementine.* Hyperion, 2007.

Perkins, Mitali. *Rickshaw Girl.* Charlesbridge, 2007.

Petty, J. T. *Clemency Pogue: Fairy Killer.* Simon and Schuster, 2005.

Pfeffer, Susan. *Life as We Knew It.* Harcourt, 2006.

Philbrick, Rodman. *The Young Man and the Sea.* Scholastic, 2004.

Pratchett, Terry. *The Amazing Maurice and His Educated Rodents.* HarperCollins, 2001.

————. *The Wee Free Men: A Story of Discworld.* HarperCollins, 2003.

Pullman, Philip. *I Was a Rat!* Knopf, 2000.

————. *The Scarecrow and His Servant.* Knopf, 2004.

Rallison, Janette. *All's Fair in Love, War, and High School.* Walker, 2003.

Resau, Laura. *Red Glass.* Delacorte, 2007.

Riordan, Rick. *The Lightning Thief.* Hyperion, 2005.

Ritter, John H. *The Boy Who Saved Baseball.* Philomel, 2003.

Roberts, Diane. *Made You Look.* Delacorte, 2003.

Ryan, Pam Muñoz. *Becoming Naomi León.* Scholastic, 2004.

————. *Esperanza Rising.* Scholastic, 2000.

————. *Paint the Wind.* Scholastic, 2007.

Sachar, Louis. *Small Steps.* Delacorte, 2006.

Sage, Angie. *My Haunted House.* HarperCollins, 2006.

Salisbury, Graham. *Eyes of the Emperor.* Wendy Lamb, 2005.

————. *Night of the Howling Dogs.* Wendy Lamb, 2007.

Schmidt, Gary D. *The Wednesday Wars.* Clarion, 2007.

Schwartz, Virginia Frances. *4 Kids in 5E and 1 Crazy Year.* Holiday House, 2006.

Scieszka, Jon. *See You Later, Gladiator.* Viking, 2000.

Shahan, Sherry. *Death Mountain.* Peachtree, 2005.

Shalant, Phyllis. *The Great Cape Rescue.* Dutton, 2007.

Shusterman, Neal. *Dread Locks.* Dutton, 2005.

————. *Unwind.* Simon and Schuster, 2007.

Smelcer, John. *The Trap.* Holt, 2006.

Smith, D. James. *The Boys of San Joaquin.* Atheneum, 2005.

Smith, Roland. *Peak.* Harcourt, 2007.

Soto, Gary. *Afterlife.* Harcourt, 2003.

————. *Worlds Apart: Traveling with Fernie and Me.* Putnam, 2005.

Spinelli, Jerry. *Stargirl.* Knopf, 2000.

Springer, Nancy, ed. *Ribbiting Tales: Original Stories about Frogs.* Philomel, 2000.

Staples, Suzanne Fisher. *The Green Dog.* Farrar Straus Giroux, 2003.

Stewart, Trenton Lee. *The Mysterious Benedict Society.* Little, Brown, 2007.

Thomas, Jane Resh. *Blind Mountain.* Clarion, 2006.

Van Draanen, Wendelin. *Sammy Keyes and the Wild Things.* Knopf, 2007.

Vernon, Ursula. *Nurk: The Strange, Surprising Adventures of a (Somewhat) Brave Shrew.* Harcourt, 2008.

Voake, Steve. *Daisy Dawson Is On Her Way!* Candlewick, 2008.

Weaver, Will. *Memory Boy.* HarperCollins, 2001.

Weeks, Sarah. *Oggie Cooder.* Scholastic, 2008.

———. *So. B. It.* HarperCollins, 2004.

Werlin, Nancy. *The Rules of Survival.* Dial, 2006.

Winerip, Michael. *Adam Canfield of the Slash.* Candlewick, 2005.

Winthrop, Elizabeth. *The Red-Hot Rattoons.* Holt, 2003.

Wolfson, Jill. *Home, and Other Big, Fat Lies.* Holt, 2006.

Wooding, Chris. *Poison.* Orchard, 2003.

Woodson, Jacqueline. *Feathers.* Putnam, 2007.

———. *Hush.* Putnam, 2002.

———. *Miracle's Boys.* Putnam, 2000.

Yep, Laurence. *The Earth Dragon Awakes: The San Francisco Earthquake of 1906.* HarperCollins, 2006.

Ylvisaker, Anne. *Little Klein.* Candlewick, 2007.

Yolen, Jane, and Robert J. Harris. *Girl in a Cage.* Philomel, 2002.

Zusak, Markus. *The Book Thief.* Knopf, 2006.

# The Read-Alouds

**Abrams, Peter.** *Down the Rabbit Hole.* HarperCollins, 2005. 375 p.
Gr. 5–8. Thirteen-year-old Ingrid lands the plum role of Alice in the Echo Falls production of *Alice in Wonderland.* She also finds herself investigating a murder. When Ingrid gets lost after soccer practice, an eccentric woman named Cracked-Up Kate invites her home and calls for a cab. Shortly afterward, Kate is found dead. Ingrid panics. She wasn't supposed to be at Kate's house, and she left her soccer shoes there. The police are looking for anyone who came in contact with Kate. Ingrid gets further tangled in the case when she starts hanging out with the son of the police chief. There are a few tricky passages to read because they are written as instant messages. This is the first book in the author's Echo Falls series.

10-Minute Selection: Tell the audience that Ingrid had left her soccer shoes at a murder scene, and she is trying to break in to retrieve them. Read the end of chapter 7, beginning with the line, "Ingrid knelt by the basement window, examined the grate." Read chapter 8. Ingrid is inside of Cracked-Up Kate's house when she hears footsteps. She hides under a bed and sees a man approach the bed. "A gloved hand appeared long and narrow, feeling under the bed." Read until the sentence, "The silence went on and on."

**Anderson, Laurie Halse.** *Fever 1793.* Simon and Schuster, 2000. 243 p.
Gr. 5–8. Fourteen-year-old Mattie lives a busy but good life, helping her mother run the Cook Coffeehouse in Philadelphia. Mattie's world is turned upside down when her mother becomes sick. Several people flee the city for the country to escape the yellow fever. Mattie learns that "more than half the city has fled, twenty thousand," and that more than three thousand people have died. Robbers destroy

the coffeehouse, her mother goes missing, and her grandfather passes away. Mattie finds herself alone in the city.

10-Minute Selection: Begin with a selection from chapter 11, "September 7th, 1793." Start with the line, "I woke when the wheels stopped turning." Mattie and her grandfather are abandoned on the side of the road for fear they have the sickness. They are ten miles from town, and Grandfather is in no condition to walk. Continue reading the short chapter 8, "September 8th, 1793." Mattie tries to find food and water for Grandfather. Continue reading chapter 13, "September 10th, 1793." Mattie and Grandfather are still trying to survive. No one helps them. "Go away. . . . We have children in here. We can't help you if you have the fever." Mattie becomes dizzy. The passage ends with her fainting.

**Archer, Lily. *The Poison Apples*. Feiwel and Friends, 2007. 288 p.**
Gr. 7–10. Three girls each find themselves with new stepmothers. Alice's famous-author father marries a popular stage actress. Reena's father marries a woman twenty-eight years his junior and only ten years older than Reena. Molly's father marries a former prom and homecoming queen who thinks her new stepdaughter is too much of a nerd. All three girls find themselves detached from their new families and attend a Massachusetts boarding school. Over a period of time, they discover they have this in common and form the Poison Apples club, based on the Snow White fairy tale. They help each other plot revenge against their evil stepmothers.

10-Minute Selection: Read the club members' prologue to the stepmothers of the world. The Poison Apples acknowledge that there are many good stepmothers in the world, but this book is about their "Incredibly Evil Stepmothers." They end the prologue with the statement, "To the bad stepmothers. You have been warned." Move to the end of part 1, chapter 13. Start with the line, "'Behold,' she said, and held out her hand. 'The Poison Apple,'" and read to the end of the chapter. The girls officially start their club. The last short section begins a few pages into chapter 6 of part 2 with the sentence, "THE TURKEY IS BURNING!" During her visit home, Alice burns the turkey, which enrages her stepmother, Rachel. When Rachel accuses Alice of being spoiled, Alice no longer has any hesitation to carry out her Poison Apples mission. End with Alice's line, "I was going to take what was dearest to her and ruin it, irrevocably and forever."

**Armstrong, Alan. *Whittington*. Random House, 2005. 191 p.**
Gr. 3–6. A tomcat named Whittington arrives at a barn full of older, rescued farm animals and asks if he can move in with them. He does so and, over the course of the year, relates the story of his extraordinary ancestor to the duck, horses, roosters, chickens, rats, and two human children—Abby and Ben—who have the ability to talk to the animals. Ben also has a reading problem, and the farm animals

decide to help him. "'So now you have one word already,' said the cat, who had no idea how many words there were but realized it was going to take more than a morning to get this boy reading half as well as his sister."

10-Minute Selection: Read the opening chapter, "Whittington Meets the Lady." Whittington introduces himself to the duck in charge of the barn. He informs her that he wants friends and that he's also a good ratter: "It's my specialty." Move to chapter 7, "Havey and the Cat's Surprise." Havey is a dog who constantly bothers the barn animals. Whittington works out a plan with Lady to teach Havey a lesson. "Havey had rushed the cat a couple of times too and sent him up a tree, but it was her daily assaults on the Lady that made the cat mad." The resulting fight leaves both the cat and dog minus patches of hair.

### Auch, Mary Jane. *I Was a Third Grade Spy.* Holiday House, 2001. 86 p.

Gr. K–4. Brian's dog, Arful, learns how to talk to humans. Brian and his friends try hard not to let other humans know their secret. "If you tell people about it, they'll take him away from Brian so they can do testing on him." The boys do, however, take advantage of Arful's gift. They send him to spy on the girls to learn their secrets. They also decide to use Arful as a ventriloquist act for the school talent show. Arful turns out to have better jokes than the boys. "Why did the dog chase the cat? . . . To get a little catnip. Get it? The dog nips the cat?" This is one of three books about Arful, the talking dog.

10-Minute Selection: Read the second half of chapter 5, beginning with the sentence, "Hi, Brian!" Emily makes a bet with the boys that if her act wins the talent show, the girls get to order the boys around for a week. Skip ahead and read chapter 7. The boys send Arful into the girls' clubhouse to learn what they're going to do for the talent show. Arful hears the word *dance*. Continue reading chapter 8. Arful reports his findings to the boys. However, he forgets the word *dance*. "'Well, there was something like ants. That's not the word, though.' 'Was it pants?' I asked. 'Plants? Slants?'" The boys figure the word was *France* and that the girls are going to make a soufflé.

### Avi. *Ereth's Birthday.* HarperCollins, 2000. 180 p.

Gr. 1–6. Ereth, an unintentionally funny-talking porcupine, constantly complains about life. A few of his many memorable phrases include, "Move over, you pie-bald pooper snoopers," "chewed over cow cuds," and "suffocating snake slime." Ereth unexpectedly finds himself taking care of three fox kits after their mother dies. This proves to be a difficult task, especially since the foxes are carnivores, and Ereth isn't. There's danger all around them in the form of human traps and a stalking fisher named Marty.

10-Minute Selection: Read the opening chapter, "A Special Day." Ereth is upset when his mice friends Poppy and Rye aren't around to celebrate his birthday.

He shouts at their eleven children. "Why don't you stuff your tiny tail into your puny gullet and gag yourself before I flip you into some skunk-cabbage sauce and turn you into a pother of butterfly plunk?" This outburst causes the young mice "to howl with glee" and makes Ereth head deeper into the forest. Next, read chapter 3, "Marty the Fisher." Marty prides himself on his hunting skills. "And of all the forest and woodland animals Marty hunted, it was porcupines he enjoyed hunting the most." He learned how to attack from below, where a porcupine had no quills. Marty spots Ereth ambling through the woods. The passage ends with "From that moment, Marty the Fisher began to stalk Ereth."

**Avi. *The Secret School*. Harcourt, 2001. 153 p.**
Gr. 3–6. It's April 1925. Miss Fletcher, the teacher of a rural one-room schoolhouse, must leave the state to care for her ailing mother. Mr. Jordan, the head of the school board, announces the school will be closed for the rest of the year. Eighth-grader Ida is worried; she won't be able to take her final exams and move on to high school. She hopes to one day become a teacher. She and the other students vote to secretly continue meeting at the school with Ida as the teacher. Ida worries Mr. Jordan will find out what the students are doing and ruin her dreams.

10-Minute Selection: Read the opening chapter. We learn right away that fourteen-year-old, four-feet-eleven Ida has a lot of determination by steering the family Model T while her seven-year-old brother pushes the brake and clutch pedals on the car floor. Miss Fletcher and Mr. Jordan tell the students that they will have a long summer vacation. Your audience will react along with Ida when Mr. Jordan states, "I'm not sure a girl needs a high school education." Read most of chapter 4, when the students vote to keep going with Ida stepping in as the teacher. Start with the line, "We've got to plan for when Miss Fletcher goes," and read to the end of the chapter with the line, "'I'm going to be scared,' Ida answered softly. 'Very scared.'"

**Avi. *The Traitor's Gate*. Atheneum, 2007. 353 p.**
Gr. 4–8. With a nod to Charles Dickens, Avi spins a fast-paced, multicharacter mystery set in nineteenth-century London. Young John Huffman is sent home from school in time to see his family's possessions taken for his father's debts. Indeed, John's father is not forthcoming in telling the truth about his financial difficulties. As John sets out to learn the true story, he finds it hard to trust his family's servant, the local bailiff, his sister's suitor, his strict teacher, and others. It turns out the government is trying to trap spies in a "traitor's gate." As the local inspector says, "[T]he thing about spies is that they prowl aimlessly about, but if there's a useful gate *open* to them, they'll pass on through."

10-Minute Selection: Read the first chapter, "I Introduce Myself." John is attending class. His teacher is a one-legged, former military man named Sergeant

Muldspoon. The boys call him Old Moldy. John falls asleep in class and is punished. The chapter ends with a cliff-hanger when John's family's servant bursts into the classroom stating, "Did you not hear me, Master John? . . . You must come now! Something perfectly dreadful has occurred."

**Barrows, Annie.** *Ivy and Bean and the Ghost That Had to Go.* **Chronicle, 2006. 125 p.**
Gr. K–3. Ivy is "the quietest kid in the class." Bean is the most rambunctious. The two get along fabulously. Ivy makes up a story that a ghost lives in the school's girls' bathroom. Soon, all of the kids believe her story. The teachers become very irritated with the children's behavior. Ivy and Bean decide to make a special potion to make the ghost go away. The girls apply the solution, along with some special gifts for the ghost, causing the toilet to overflow. This is the second book in the Ivy and Bean series.

10-Minute Selection: Read the first two chapters. We learn that Ivy makes up the ghost story to draw attention from the fact that she cannot do a cartwheel. She tells the Gymnastics Club, "'We've got an emergency situation going on. Right over there.' . . . She was pointing directly to the girls' bathroom." Bean reminds Ivy they took an oath to tell each other everything. (They had balked at the idea of a blood oath and a booger oath and finally settled for a spit oath.) Move on to the chapter titled "Sneaky Bean." One of the ingredients the girls need for their potion is "the hair of an enemy." After a funny shouting exchange with her older sister Nancy, Bean sneaks into Nancy's bedroom and begins to "snip very, very quietly."

**Bauer, Joan.** *Hope Was Here.* **Putnam, 2000. 186 p.**
Gr. 6–12. Hope is a teenage waitress who moves with her aunt from Brooklyn to Mulhoney, Wisconsin. They work in the Welcome Stairways Diner for G.T. Stoop, who is fighting corruption in the town by running for mayor. One of the many strikes G.T. has against him is that he has been diagnosed with leukemia. Hope and other concerned citizens rally around G.T. to get him elected. In G.T., Hope eventually finds the father figure she's been in search of for years.

10-Minute Selection: Read the last third of chapter 11. Begin reading with the sentence, "The last hour on my shift and it had truly been one of those days," and continue to the end of the chapter. The race for mayor has taken a nasty turn. A woman screams that she found a mouse in her salad at the Welcome Stairways Diner. Skip ahead and read chapter 13. Three thugs beat up Braverman, the young grill man from the diner. They warn him that he "better shut [his] mouth about politics in this town." The violence only makes the local youth fight harder to get G.T. elected. End with the sentences, "Spend some time in Wisconsin. We'll blow your socks off."

**Bauer, Joan.** *Peeled.* **Putnam, 2008. 247 p.**
Gr. 6–12. Hildy lives in an upstate rural New York community where the apple orchards have had two years of bad harvest. The town of Banesville gets a lot of attention due to mysterious incidents at a local haunted house. The editor of the local paper exploits these occurrences, sometimes crossing the line of journalistic integrity. Developers make plans to buy up some of the ailing orchards. Hildy knows that something rotten is going on and uses her position as reporter for the high school newspaper to get to the truth. Unfortunately, the school paper shuts down when it is threatened with a lawsuit.

10-Minute Selection: Read the first chapter. It opens with the attention-grabbing line, "Bonnie Sue Bomgartner, Banesville's soon-to-be 67th Apple Blossom Queen, let loose with a stream of projectile vomiting in the high school cafeteria." Hildy is pressured to write only copy that emphasizes the positive aspects of the apple festival. Local talk moves on to the spooky signs that "appear on the front door of the old Ludlow house," such as "Danger to all ye who enter" and "The Domicile of Doom." The chapter ends with Hildy remembering the advice of her late reporter father: "'When a story keeps coming at you day and night, pay attention.' . . . The phone call came in early September. I'm here to tell you, I paid attention."

**Bauer, Marion Dane.** *The Double-Digit Club.* **Holiday House, 2004. 116 p.**
Gr. 3–5. Nine-year-old Sarah is devastated when her best friend, Paige, joins the Double-Digit Club on her tenth birthday. The Double-Digit Club was created by Valerie Miller for girls in school when they turn ten years old. Club members are forbidden from socializing with younger girls. Sarah and Paige had pledged to each other to turn down Valerie's invitation, but Paige caves under peer pressure. Sarah steals a neighbor's antique doll in an effort to lure Paige back. The doll breaks during an argument, and Sarah finds herself caught in a moral dilemma. Sarah later learns the real reason Paige joined the Double-Digit Club has to do with Sarah herself.

10-Minute Selection: Read chapter 2, "Say It!" It's Paige's tenth birthday, and she and Sarah head for the beach. They know a confrontation with the Double-Digit Club is inevitable and practice Paige's refusal. The members of the Double-Digit Club surprise them by having a birthday cake ready for Paige. Valerie starts talking about their plans that afternoon. Paige will join the other members of the club at the movie theater that Valerie's father owns. Sarah expectantly waits for Paige to respond. "She turned to Paige. *Say it,* her eyes commanded. *Just like we agreed. Say it!*" Paige doesn't say a word as she brushes past Sarah and sits with the other girls. The chapter ends with Sarah walking away from the girls' laughter.

**Birdsall, Jeanne.** *The Penderwicks: A Summer Tale of Four Sisters, Two Rabbits, and a Very Interesting Boy.* **Knopf, 2005. 262 p.**
Gr. 3–6. The four Penderwick sisters—Rosalind, Sky, Jane, and Batty—normally spend summer vacation on Cape Cod. Circumstances make their father look elsewhere. He locates a place on the Arundel estate. The owner, Mrs. Tifton, is a fairly cold person, but the girls and their dog, Hound, have a summer's worth of adventures. They quickly become friends with Mrs. Tifton's son Jeffrey. The whole vacation is threatened when Mrs. Tifton and her boyfriend try to send Jeffrey to the Pencey Military Academy, where "Boys Become Men and Men Become Soldiers." The sequel is titled *The Penderwicks on Gardam Street.*

10-Minute Selection: Introduce the characters by stating the four Penderwick sisters are exploring the estate of young Jeffrey and that the youngest sister, Batty, likes to wear costume butterfly wings. Read chapter 5, "A New Hero." Batty wanders into an enclosure that contains a large bull. "Not only was it still there, it had come a step closer. It was only fifteen feet away. 'Nice horsie,' said Batty hopefully." The other children spring into action to save Batty from the charging bull.

**Birney, Betty G.** *The Seven Wonders of Sassafras Springs.* **Atheneum, 2005. 210 p.**
Gr. 3–5. This was my favorite book of 2005, when I served on the Newbery Award Committee. It spoke to me because of the storytelling element in the book. Eben reads about the seven man-made wonders of the world and wishes aloud that he could visit them. His father asks him to define a "Wonder," which he does. "Here it is. It says, 'a marvel; that which arouses awe, astonishment, surprise, or admiration.'" His father then states, "[T]here's no use searching the world for Wonders when you can't see the marvels right under your own nose." He promises to reward Eben with a trip to Colorado if Eben finds "Seven Wonders right here in Sassafras Springs." Eben finds them and, in doing so, learns a story behind each fairly modest wonder.

10-Minute Selection: Read the second half of the chapter "Day Two: Jeb Joins In," beginning with the sentence, "'If you're going back up the Ridge, the next stop after the Pritchards' is Cully Pone's.'" Finish this chapter and read the entire following chapter, "The Rainmaker's Revenge: Cully Pone's Story." It is a bigger-than-life tale of a rainmaker who does his job too well and floods out the town of Garnerville, fifty miles to the north. The "Wonder" in this story is a plain-looking bookcase that also serves as a boat for the rainmaker.

**Bledsoe, Lucy Jane.** *Hoop Girlz.* **Holiday House, 2002. 162 p.**
Gr. 4–5. Eleven-year-old River is depressed when she doesn't make the A-Team for a big basketball tournament. She had hopes of becoming the team's most valuable

player (MVP). The coach promised all of the girls that the A-Team's MVP will meet WNBA star Emily Hargraves, River's idol. Instead, River assembles her own ragtag B-Team, including Jennifer, a wheelchair-bound athlete with deadly aim. River also recruits her older brother Zack to coach them. They call themselves the Hoop Girlz and work hard to make it to the tournament, learning how to have fun in the process.

10-Minute Selection: Start well into chapter 10 with the sentence, "'Hey!' Kammie blurted. 'River has an A-Team jersey,'" and finish the chapter. River is asked to leave the Hoop Girlz and play for the A-Team. She accepts but changes her mind and sticks with her true team. River then seeks permission to hold team practice in the ballroom of a haunted mansion. Continue reading the entire chapter 11 as the local sheriff, Jennifer's father, gets permission for the girls to practice in the mansion. He not only recruits the fire department to haul in a portable basketball hoop but he also convinces the firefighters to scrimmage against the girls.

**Blume, Judy. *Soupy Saturdays with the Pain and the Great One*. Delacorte, 2007. 108 p.**
Gr. K–3. Jake's sister, Abigail, calls him the Pain "because that's what he is. He's a first grade pain. And he will always be a pain—even if he lives to be a hundred." Jake calls his third-grader sister the Great One "because she thinks she's so great." The two narrate their own chapters about themselves, their friends, their family, and each other. The two are featured in the picture book *The Pain and the Great One*. This is the first chapter book to feature the siblings.

10-Minute Selection: Share the chapter featuring the Pain titled "Soccer Doc." Jake is a goalie, but soccer's no fun, because the other team scores a lot. Jake wants to play other positions. His friend Justin, coach Soccer Doc's son, isn't having fun either. He wants to play goalie. The Great One tells the two boys to simply tell their coach. Justin isn't sure it's that easy. "'Duh . . .' the Great One said. 'How is he supposed to know if you don't tell him?'" Follow this by reading the chapter titled "Party Girl," a selection featuring Abigail. Abigail decides to have a half-birthday sleepover party. Unfortunately, the Pain gets sick, and only one girl, Emily, shows up. Emily is not crazy about the color pink or being a princess. She is also not ready for a sleepover. Jake comes downstairs and takes one of the princess tiaras as his own crown.

**Bowe, Julie. *My Last Best Friend*. Harcourt, 2007. 146 p.**
Gr. 3–5. Ida May's best friend, Elizabeth, moved away and stopped writing even though the two vowed to be friends forever. Ida May vows to never have another best friend. Instead, she puts up with mean-girl Jenna because Ida May's mother is convinced that Jenna is a nice girl. She is anything but nice. Jenna calls Ida May

"I-duh" and mocks her in front of others. A new girl, Stacey, moves to town and shows interest in befriending Ida May. Jenna tries to convince Stacey that Ida May isn't worth her time. It soon becomes evident to Ida May that Stacey has a secret and is not who she says she is. The sequel is titled *My New Best Friend*.

10-Minute Selection: Read chapter 1. We are introduced to the unique voice of Ida May. "In fourth grade you start to smell funny. So you get your first stick of deodorant. . . . You rub some on. After five tries you finally hit your armpit." Ida May's first encounter with Stacey is hilarious because Ida May is caught with eight pieces of Choco-chunks in her mouth. Move on to chapter 3. Ida May and Stacey are in the school lunchroom. The girls notice that a boy is shooting spit wads at them. Stacey walks up to the boy and announces, "You like me, don't you," at the top of her voice. She throws her arm around the boy, making him turn red with embarrassment. Ida May watches and wonders "how a person with six spitballs stuck in her hair can do something like that."

**Bowler, Tim.** *Storm Catchers.* **Margaret K. McElderry, 2001. 200 p.**
Gr. 6–10. Ella has been kidnapped by a large, hulking man. He leaves a note: "Tell a soul and she's dead. We'll be in touch." The man turns out to be a huge teenage boy who hides her in a cave under an abandoned lighthouse. Ella's older brother, Finn, feels guilty because he should have been home watching over her. The kidnapper calls and directs Finn to be the one to bring the money. At the same time, their younger brother, Sam, is communicating with a strange, ghostly girl who appears only to him. The girl constantly warns Sam that a storm is coming, and she lures him out of bed to follow her outside. All of the events in this fast-paced thriller lead to a disturbing family secret.

10-Minute Selection: Read chapter 1, which opens with the actual kidnapping. Ella is alone in the house with Sam. Their parents are out, and Finn has snuck out to be with his friend. Ella hears a strange tapping noise downstairs. She investigates and freezes in horror. "Reflected in the glass was a figure standing behind her in the doorway." She eludes him at first, but he eventually overpowers her and takes her away.

**Broach, Elise.** *Shakespeare's Secret.* **Holt, 2005. 243 p.**
Gr. 4–8. Hero and her sister, Beatrice, were named after characters in the Shakespeare play *Much Ado about Nothing*. Their family has just moved into a new home that is the subject of local interest. "You know, Hero, when you meet your classmates tomorrow, if you need something to break the ice, you might tell them you're living in the Murphy diamond house. That will make you something of a celebrity." The gem in question is a seventeen-carat diamond that folks believe is hidden somewhere on the property. Hero, her new friend Danny, and her neighbor Mrs. Roth find clues to where the diamond may be hidden. Along the way,

Hero learns about theories of Shakespeare's true identity and how he may have been related to the previous owner of Hero's house. More shocking is the discovery of the true relationship between Danny and Mrs. Roth.

10-Minute Selection: Read chapter 2. Hero meets Mrs. Roth and learns a little of the Murphy diamond-house story. She promises to return after school the next day to learn about the details. This will be enough to tantalize your listeners. Continue with chapter 3. Hero does not have a good first day at her new school. When she tells the class her name, a girl shouts out, "Hey, that's my dog's name." Hero is subjected to barking noises the rest of the day.

**Bruchac, Joseph. *Bearwalker.* HarperCollins, 2007. 208 p.**
Gr. 5–8. The opening passage sets the tone for this exciting, suspenseful page-turner. A journal entry states, "I'm not bleeding so much now. I have to keep my eyes and ears open. Otherwise he might creep up on me." The prologue also includes a Mohawk legend about the Bearwalker, a monstrous bear who takes the shape of a man to lure humans to their death. This sets up the story of eighth-grader Baron, a frequent target of bullies and a member of the Mohawk Bear Clan. He and his classmates take a school trip to Camp Chuckamuck in the Adirondacks. The campers are soon faced with danger when they are isolated from the outside world and learn that the camp staff members aren't who they pretend to be. What's worse, an actual Bearwalker might be in the area.

10-Minute Selection: Read chapter 20, "Battery." Baron is caught between a mother bear and her cubs. In fact, the bears are playing with Baron, batting at him with their paws and pulling at his clothes with their teeth. The mother bear comes over, bites Baron, and tosses him to the side. Continue reading the next chapter, "Still." Jason Jones, the Bearwalker, is hunting Baron. The chapter ends with the line, "A bloody hand grasps my arm."

**Bruchac, Joseph. *The Dark Pond.* HarperCollins, 2004. 142 p.**
Gr. 6–10. Armie, a half-Armenian, half-Shawnee boy, is very comfortable around birds and animals. He transfers to the North Mountains School in the wilderness. He discovers a pond a few miles away from campus. Something in the pond calls to him, trying to lure him to his death. A Native American named Mitch works with Armie to try to kill the monster that inhabits the pond.

10-Minute Selection: Read the first page of chapter 2. It starts with the line, "The first time I saw the dark pond was on one of my walks," and lets the audience know that the main character attends a wilderness school. Skip ahead a few pages and pick up with the sentence, "The ice hadn't thawed yet, and so I thought it would be safe to walk across it." Finish the chapter and continue reading the entire chapter 3. Armie encounters a fox that behaves strangely. Armie learns that the fox is actually drawing him away from the pond. Once he's safely away from the pond, Armie looks back and sees a chilling sight: several animal and bird tracks heading down the slope. "All those tracks led out onto the pond. Not one track came back again."

**Buckley, Michael.** *The Sisters Grimm, Book One: The Fairy Tale Detectives.* **Amulet, 2005. 284 p.**
Gr. 4–8. Sabrina and Daphne learn that they are the great-great-great-great-granddaughters of the brothers Grimm and that all of the popular fairy-tale characters are still alive. These famous characters are now known as the "Everafters," and they live in Ferryport Landing (aka Fairy Port), near the Hudson River in New York. Sabrina and Daphne move in with their grandmother and learn about their destiny. They are dismayed to learn that many of the Everafters would like to see the entire Grimm family dead. This is the first book in the Sisters Grimm series.

10-Minute Selection: Read the end of chapter 3, when three hoodlums threaten the Grimms. Start with the sentence, "'Well, hello, ladies,' a voice said as three men emerged from the deep shadows that lined the pathway to the parking lot." Continue reading the entire chapter 4. Skinny, old Mr. Canis surprises the girls when he easily handles the three tough men. The girls then get the low-down about several of their favorite storybook characters, such as Jack. "Jack robbed many giants and killed quite a number of them, too. In his day, he was rich and famous, though I hear he's working at a Big and Tall clothing store downtown, now." A giant kidnaps Mrs. Grimm and Mr. Canis. The passage ends, "'Where are you going?' 'I'm going to rescue our family,' the little girl called back without stopping."

**Byars, Betsy.** *Keeper of the Doves.* **Viking, 2002. 121 p.**
Gr. 4–8. "Another girl? Not another girl? Don't tell me I've got another daughter?" That new baby girl is Amen McBee, also known as Amie, the narrator of this story. Her four sisters are Abigail, Augusta, Arabella, and Annabella. Amen loves words and writes poems. She's delighted by visits from her grandmother and uncle. She's also curious about the reclusive Mr. Tominski, who lives near the house. Amen's twin sisters describe Mr. Tominski as an evil man, but the girls' father tells them the story of how Mr. Tominski saved his life. Things get ugly when the family finds their dog, Scout, injured. The twins blame Mr. Tominski.

10-Minute Selection: Read the funny chapter 3, "Children!" Aunt Pauline lives with the family, and she is called "unkindly." She tells the twins, "If you make ugly faces, children, your face will freeze like that," to which innocent four-year-old Amen says, "Is that what happened to your face, Aunt Pauline?" Aunt Pauline leaves in a huff, and the twins have fun imitating her. Move to chapter 11, "Keeper of the Doves." It is the first time Amen and her grandmother see Mr. Tominski.

They quietly observe him holding pennies and letting the doves take them out of his hand. Grandmama is quite taken by what she has seen. "The man is a dove magician."

**Byars, Betsy. *Me Tarzan*. HarperCollins, 2000. 87 p.**
Gr. 2–5. Dorothy surprises everyone by getting the role of Tarzan in the class play. She can deliver an amazing Tarzan yell. Her yell is so great that it attracts real animals whenever she lets it loose. She usually gets inspired to yell when she begins "to smell the jungle and feel the lush tropical vines." At one point, the schoolyard is filled with "dogs and cats as well as seven horses from the Friendly Riding Academy. . . . Apparently there is also an iguana." Dorothy's yell even makes a small child wet his pants. Trouble brews when her yell attracts all the animals from a neighboring circus to the school play. Have fun doing your own Tarzan yell while reading Dorothy's lines. Ask your listeners to yell with you.

10-Minute Selection: Read the opening chapter, "Bring Tarzan." Dorothy tells her mother that she got the role of Tarzan over her "enemy," Dwayne Wiggert. She sends a parting note to him that reads, "Me Tarzan, you Dwayne." Read chapter 3, "Almost Like an Elephant." Dorothy once again does her Tarzan yell. Two dogs and a cat show up in her front yard. "And then—and then there was a trumpeting sound, almost like an elephant."

**Byars, Betsy, Betsy Duffey, and Laurie Myers. *The SOS File*. Holt, 2004. 73 p.**
Gr. 1–4. Mr. Magro's latest extra-credit writing assignment is for kids to describe a time in their lives when they needed help. Liz describes the time her go-cart, the Pink Panther, raced uncontrollably down the street, injuring Liz (a pulled muscle and eight stitches) and her friend Marcie (scrapes). "A little kid ran over and stared at me . . . and said, 'Do it again.'" Kyle has three SOS's in his hilarious story about getting stung by yellow jackets, having his face swell up, and then finding himself trapped in the girls' bathroom. Brianna uses the pen name "Ima Writer" to describe her dangerous episode of nearly drowning in a river. In the end, Mr. Magro reads his own story about being held back in first grade because he had dyslexia.

10-Minute Selection: Read the heartwarming chapter titled "Miracle on Main Street by Joy Frazure." Joy was found in a dumpster when she was a newborn. Later, with the help of her adopted parents, they searched for the man who rescued her. Next, read the funny chapter titled "Mrs. Meany by Robbie Robertson." Robby acquires a goat named Billy. The goat wanders into a mean neighbor's cornfield. Robbie is trying to save his goat when he says, "'Be quiet or the old hag will—' At that moment, the corn parted, and there stood the old hag." Robbie faints. Mrs. Meany turns to the goat and asks, "Well, do you think he needs mouth-to-mouth resuscitation?"

**Cabot, Meg.** *Jinx.* **HarperCollins, 2007. 262 p.**

Gr. 6–10. Jean Honeychurch moves from Iowa to Manhattan to live with her well-to-do relatives. Her nickname is Jinx. "I'm a bad luck magnet. In fact, since birth, wherever I am . . . well, things always seem to go screwy." We eventually learn that the reason she moved was to escape her ex-boyfriend, who became overly obsessed with her. Jean may have witchcraft powers; her ancestor was burned as a witch. Jean's cousin Tory believes that Jean inherited their descendant's powers. Tory wants them for herself, even if it means going to dangerous extremes.

10-Minute Selection: Read chapter 12, which opens with the line, "It started the next day." What "starts" is Tory's personal, vindictive war against Jean. Jean approaches her school locker. In it, "hanging by a shoelace from the vent in the top half of my locker door, was a dead rat." The rat turns out to be from the school's biology lab. Jean knows what Tory is doing isn't real magic, but she thinks about a protection spell to keep her and others safe "from the kind of dangerous pranks Tory and her friends liked to perform." The chapter ends with the prophetic line, "But things can't get any worse, can they?"

**Cameron, Ann.** *Gloria's Way.* **Farrar Straus Giroux, 2000. 96 p.**

Gr. K–3. Six interconnected stories follow Gloria, her family, and friends Julian, Huey, and Latisha. In one story, Latisha is mean to the other kids, and they retaliate by dumping a pie on her steps. Julian's father helps the kids do the right thing. Two stories are about Huey's dog, Spunky. The kids try to teach Spunky commands, but the dog becomes obsessed with chasing squirrels. "It was when we got to 'Stay!' that the squirrels made fun of him." In one story, Gloria worries about her true friendship with Julian, and in another story, Gloria is frustrated by fractions. "Fractions are phony!" She gets help from her father on a rare evening alone with him. Gloria appears in other Cameron books about her and her friends Julian and Huey.

10-Minute Selection: Read the opening chapter, "A Valentine for My Mother." Gloria works very hard on a special valentine, complete with red-paper double doors and the message, "I love you like the sky but more." She sets it outside on the doorknob, but the wind carries it into a neighbor's parrot's cage. Gloria tries to retrieve the valentine but is scared of the parrot. Gloria is crushed when the parrot ruins the valentine. Mr. Bates helps her come up with an alternate solution. The young audience will enjoy hearing the parrot's dialogue.

**Carter, Alden.** *Love, Football, and Other Contact Sports.* **Holiday House, 2006. 261 p.**

Gr. 6–11. This collection of short stories focuses on the football players of Argyle West High School as well as their family and friends. The stories are grouped by sophomore, junior, and senior years. Different characters act as narrators. One of the stories, "The Briefcase," features a non-jock narrator. Chad is worried he'll be picked on for carrying a briefcase instead of a backpack to school. Another highlight is "The Doughnut Boots His Reputation," which features a huge offensive tackle who attends baby classes and learns how to change a diaper.

10-Minute Selection: Although many of the stories make great stand-alone reads, if you have time for only one chapter, choose "A Girl's Guide to Football Players," written by "the female editorial staff of the *Purple Cow Literary Magazine.*" The piece takes a look at the type of boy who plays each position and what kind of car each typically drives. Follow this with the brief "Football Player's Guide to Love," which consists of "Love. Well, you see it's, uh, sort of, you know, kinda like when . . . Hey, can we talk about this later?"

**Clements, Andrew. *Jake Drake, Class Clown*. Simon and Schuster, 2002. 72 p.** Gr. 1–5. Jake recalls his second-grade experience with Miss Bruce, a student teacher. Miss Bruce never smiles. Her teaching strategy is to be serious and tough to maintain control of the classroom. Jake decides he's going to be the class clown. He likes the attention. He practices knock-knock jokes on his sister and makes funny faces in the mirror. One day in class, Jake starts thinking about funny noises, such as duck sounds and mouth-pops. He thinks about burps and swallows air while working on his spelling workbook. When Miss Bruce asks if he's done, he says, "'NOOOOOOOOOOOOOOOOOOOOOOOOOOOPE.' It was the longest, loudest burp of my life!" Miss Bruce loses control of the class and flees the room crying. This is one of four Jake Drake books.

10-Minute Selection: Read chapter 3, "Scared Silly." Jake hopes Miss Bruce will smile today, but he's disappointed. Miss Bruce has a spelling bee, but her strict interpretation of the rules frustrates the students; some have to sit down even if they know the correct spelling. Jake is angry when kids are humiliated. He stands up to spell *mouse*, "but something inside my head snapped. I looked right at Miss Bruce and in a high, squeaky voice I said, 'Mouse: m-i-c-k-e-y; mouse.'" When Miss Bruce says he didn't spell the right word, Jake replies in his best Mickey Mouse voice, "Heh, heh—well then, I guess I'm out." Later, Jake believes he saw a smile on Miss Bruce's face.

**Clements, Andrew. *No Talking*. Simon and Schuster, 2007. 146 p.** Gr. 3–6. The fifth-graders, known to their teachers as "the Unshushables" due to their noisy behavior, start a contest inspired by Mahatma Gandhi. The idea of bringing order to his mind through the avoidance of speech inspires Dave Parker. Soon, boys and girls compete against one another to see who can get through the next few days saying the fewest words possible. They agree to specific exceptions, such as speaking a maximum of three words when responding to teachers. This action thrills some teachers and makes others mad—including Principal

Hiatt. The experiment turns into a classic case of civil disobedience. Eventually, the whole school joins the contest. This entertaining story might inspire some kids to try it themselves.

10-Minute Selection: Read chapter 5, "The Contest," where the two ring-leaders, Dave and Lynsey, settle on the contest rules. Next, read chapter 12, "Guessing Games." The contest is on, and the various teachers learn to adapt after their initial puzzlement. Mr. Burton, the English teacher, is actually excited about the contest. He has the kids create a fun group story with each student contributing only three words.

**Clements, Andrew.** *A Week in the Woods.* **Simon and Schuster, 2002. 190 p.**
Gr. 3–6. Fifth-grader Mark is the new boy in his New Hampshire school. He's uninterested in school and makes a bad first impression with his science teacher, Mr. Maxwell. Over the course of the year, Mark matures and becomes interested in the outdoors. He participates in the school's "A Week in the Woods" program. Mark is looking at another student's Leatherman, a multi-tool device, when he is unjustly accused of bringing a knife. "And our district has a zero-tolerance rule about bringing weapons to school. So this *knife* means you are going to be sus-pended from school." Instead of riding back in Mr. Maxwell's truck, Mark takes off for the woods.

10-Minute Selection: Read chapter 19, "Here." Mark realizes Mr. Maxwell is after him and decides to go back. However, Mark is disoriented. It's getting colder outside. "I'm lost." Continue with chapter 20, "Camp." Mark quickly assesses his situation and goes into survival mode. He builds a shelter, starts a fire, and even prepares for the possibility of a bear wandering into his camp. The chapter ends with Mark hearing a hoarse voice saying, "Mark—it's okay. It's me. I need . . . help."

**Colfer, Eoin.** *Artemis Fowl.* **Hyperion, 2001. 279 p.**
Gr. 4–10. Artemis is a twelve-year-old criminal genius determined to restore his family fortune. He decides to do this by stealing gold from the fairy folk. With the help of his bodyguard, Butler, Artemis first decodes the fairies' secret Book and then kidnaps Captain Holly Short, a fairy who belongs to the LEPrecon Unit. The fairy world soon marshals its forces on Artemis, including unleashing a fear-some troll on the Fowl estate. "The manservant realized instantly what the fairies had done. They had sent a primal hunter. A creature with no interest in magic or rules. A thing that would simply kill anything in its way, regardless of species. This was the perfect predator." This is the first book in Colfer's popular series.

10-Minute Selection: Read the prologue, which briefly introduces Artemis. Next, read the last quarter of chapter 4, "Abduction." Begin with the sentence, "Butler checked the porta-radar, muting the volume in case the equipment betrayed their position," and read until the end of the chapter. Artemis and Butler spot Holly for the first time and subdue her. Holly is astonished by how much these two humans know about fairies. "Holly was dumbfounded. There was a human before her, casually spouting sacred secrets."

**Colfer, Eoin. *The Supernaturalist.* Hyperion, 2004. 267 p.**
Gr. 5–10. Cosmo Hill is an orphan trapped at the Clarissa Frayne Institute for Parentally Challenged Boys. The boys held there are subject to harmful consumer testing. Cosmo escapes but is mortally wounded. As he's dying, he sees translucent creatures apparently sucking his life force. Cosmo is rescued by three "kids" who make up a team dedicated to wiping out these Parasites. Unfortunately, most of the human population can't see the creatures and don't realize they are in danger. The plot leads to surprising facts about the Parasites and the team's corporate ally.
    10-Minute Selection: Read the first part of the opening chapter. Cosmo and the other boys have been guinea pigs for antiperspirants; some brands burn their legs. Redwood is the marshal in charge of keeping order. He's a bully. Cosmo finds an opportunity to escape with his friend Ziplock when their transport crashes. Redwood breaks his nose, and Cosmo takes advantage. "Cosmo grabbed the marshal's nose, twisting almost ninety degrees." Redwood recovers and pursues the boys to the top of a skyscraper, where he plans to kill them. Ziplock goes over the edge, taking Cosmo with him. Finish with the sentences, "His final word was to Cosmo. 'Sorry,' he said, and slipped over the edge."

**Collins, Ross. *Medusa Jones.* Scholastic, 2008. 137 p.**
Gr. 3–6. Medusa is a Gorgon. She and her family have snakes for hair and can turn people into stone. Their lawn is full of petrified postal carriers and salespeople. Medusa and her friends, Chiron the centaur and Mino the Minotaur, are teased and picked on by the bullies known as the Champions (Perseus, Theseus, and Cassandra). Medusa wants to turn them into stone, but her parents forbid it. When the kids are forced to take a field trip together to Mount Olympus, Medusa smuggles her three-headed dog, Cerberus, along. The Champions get trapped on a ledge after a rock fall. Medusa and her friends spring into action to save their tormentors.
    10-Minute Selection: Read chapter 3. Medusa is tired of being humiliated because of the snakes, and she goes to hair salon named Salon de Josef. Josef loves her hair. "'C'est magnifique!' said Monsieur Josef. 'I ave never seen their lak. So real. So . . . snakey.'" He mists and massages the snakes, but when he holds "aloft a large silver pair of scissors," the snakes attack. Move on to chapter 5. We meet Miss Medea, the kids' mean teacher. She puts Medusa and her friends in Group A with the Champions simply because she's mean and wants to see the kids tangle with one another. She lets another group go on a field trip to the very popular

Neptune's Waterworld. Every time Miss Medea mentions Neptune's Waterworld, and she does several times, Group B cheers.

**Coombs, Kate.** *The Runaway Princess.* **Farrar Straus Giroux, 2006. 279 p.**
Gr. 4–7. Princess Meg is upset when she learns that her hand in marriage is one of the prizes in a contest involving dozens of princes. Her father, the king, wants the princes to rid the land of a witch, a dragon, and bandits. Meg's first thoughts are to *save* the witch, the dragon, and the bandits. She enlists the help of friends and servants. Not only is Meg going against the wishes of her father but she also runs into an unworthy prince who finds a way to take control of the entire kingdom.

10-Minute Selection: Read the last third of chapter 4, starting with the sentence, "The woods were full of sunlight and birdsong." Meg ventures into the woods to warn the witch. She finds the witch, Gorba, in a cottage full of frogs. Gorba refuses any help and kicks Meg out. Continue reading the very last section of chapter 5, beginning with the line, "The witch sat in an overstuffed flowered armchair reading a book with a scarlet cover depicting a golden-haired maiden being rescued by a very brawny young man in armor." The witch is attacked by a group of princes. Gorba turns them into frogs. "I gave 'em fair warning, didn't I?"

**Craig, Joe.** *Jimmy Coates: Assassin?* **HarperCollins, 2005. 218 p.**
Gr. 4–8. Eleven-year-old Jimmy is shocked when men come to his house and demand he comes with them. He soon learns that he isn't who he thought he was. Jimmy is a creation of the government, a robot. He's part human and part gadget: "Sixty-two percent of you is earth's finest technological hardware." He is also dismayed to learn that he was designed to kill; he's an assassin for the government. His target is a leading critic of the prime minister, someone who "spoke passionately in public, campaigning for old freedoms." This is the first in a series about Jimmy Coates.

10-Minute Selection: The book opens with lots of action. Read chapter 1, "Strange Talents." Agents show up at Jimmy's home, prompting his mother to speak. "'Run, Jimmy,' she said, gasping, her voice almost a whisper. She clutched at her throat, and then shouted, 'JIMMY, RUN!'" As he escapes, Jimmy learns he has reflexes and skills he never knew he had. The chapter ends with Jimmy crashing out of a second-story window. Move on to chapter 8, "Never Safe." Inform your audience that Jimmy is hiding out at a friend's house. Begin with the sentence, "Felix, you're here," and go to the end of the chapter. Several men chase Jimmy. He leaps into a helicopter, overpowers the pilot, and looks at the controls. "He was alone in an airborne helicopter. He gulped again, and realized there probably wasn't an instruction manual at hand."

**Creech, Sharon.** *Granny Torrelli Makes Soup.* **Joanna Cotler, 2003. 141 p.**
Gr. 4–6. Twelve-year-old Rosie's best friend is Bailey, a blind neighbor boy. The two grew up together. They have their fights, such as the time when Rosie decided to learn how to read Braille. She was surprised at Bailey's angry reaction. Granny Torrelli shares parallel stories from her childhood in the old country. When a new girl moves into the neighborhood and shows interest in Bailey, Rosie becomes extremely jealous. She's confused about her feelings toward Bailey.

10-Minute Selection: Read the two-page chapter titled "You Going to Tell Me?" as setup for the rest of the selection. Granny Torrelli asks Rosie what's wrong, and Rosie replies, "It's just that Bailey." Granny makes Rosie laugh by pretending to cry, "Boo hoo hoo. . . . That Bailey has made me molto, molto sad. Boo hoo hoo." Skip to the chapter titled "Put Your Feet Up"; read through it, the next four short chapters, and the last chapter, titled "Tutto Va Bene . . ." We learn a little of Rosie and Bailey's past growing up together. Rosie doesn't always know how to deal with Bailey's blindness, and she sometimes reacts inappropriately. Bailey is just as stubborn at times. The last chapter shows Rosie scheming to get a guide dog for Bailey. She takes what she thinks is a stray mutt, but it turns out to be someone's pet. "And that was the end of the secret guide dog business."

**Creech, Sharon.** *Heartbeat.* **HarperCollins, 2004. 192 p.**
Gr. 4–6. Twelve-year-old Annie's world is changing. Her grandfather is slowing down, her mother is pregnant, and her friend Max, who she runs with, is increasingly moody. Annie runs barefoot to help cope. She loves to run for her own enjoyment and resists pressure to join the girls' track team. Annie also loves to draw. Miss Freely, her art teacher, assigns the class to draw one hundred pictures of an apple. "Draw one hundred pictures of the same old apple?" Miss Freely responds with, "I think you will discover some interesting things. I think you will discover the un-ordinary-ness of an apple."

10-Minute Selection: Read several of the following short chapters. Some have a common thread, and a few are interesting on their own. "Fears and Loves" makes Annie think how alike and different she is from her classmates. Annie learns about footnotes and compares them to her feet. You also get to read some humorous footnotes. Read the following chapters to show how angry Annie gets when pressured to run for the school team: "The Coach," "Perspective," "Mad Max," and "Forbidden Words," which is mostly setup for the last chapter in this sequence, "Shoeless."

**Creech, Sharon.** *The Wanderer.* **HarperCollins, 2000. 305 p.**
Gr. 5–8. Sophie jumps at the chance to sail across the Atlantic Ocean with her three uncles and two male cousins. They are going to see Bompie, father of the three uncles. Their boat, *The Wanderer,* isn't the greatest boat, but they all work

together, and sometimes bicker, to make the journey successful. Each one has the task of teaching the others something new. Sophie decides to tell them Bompie's stories. Her cousin Cody teaches the others how to juggle. Sophie and Cody alternate as narrators.

10-Minute Selection: Read chapter 9, "Beheading." Sophie shows stress when killing fish, while Cody humorously mangles sailing terms to irritate the others. "Reef the rudder and heave ho, take off." Next, read chapter 14, "Bompie and the Car," the first of Sophie's Bompie stories. The story ends with Bompie being whipped by his father and fed apple pie by his mother. If time permits, read the second Bompie story, found within chapter 18, "Bompie and the Train." It, too, ends with Bompie getting whipped by his father and fed apple pie by his mother. Begin with the sentence, "But Sophie did tell us another Bompie story when we were out clamming," and read to the end of the chapter.

**Cummings, Priscilla.** *Red Kayak.* **Dutton, 2004. 208 p.**
Gr. 5–10. There's been an accident. Ben, the toddler living next door to thirteen-year-old Brady, dies when the kayak he and his mother were in sinks. Brady pulls the little boy out of the water, performs CPR, and is hailed a hero. Unfortunately, the boy dies at the hospital. Ben later learns that his two best friends, Digger and J.T., were responsible for the accident. Brady feels guilty when he covers up his friends' deeds.

10-Minute Selection: Read the last few pages of chapter 3, beginning with the line, "About a minute later, I got called down to the office." Move on to read the entire chapter 5, which describes Brady's rescue attempt. Move to chapter 8, starting at the beginning and ending on the lines, "'Let's go home.' And we did." Brady has just learned from his mother that Ben died. Read one more short passage, from the end of chapter 13, which sets up the core focus of the book. Brady realizes that his friends had drilled holes in the kayak. Begin with the sentence, "It was when I turned the corner on the boathouse and pulled the rake through a tangle of prickers that I saw something reflect the sun," and go to the end of the chapter. The object in the water that Brady finds is his father's missing cordless drill. "Did Digger have something to do with sinking the kayak?"

**Curtis, Christopher Paul.** *Elijah of Buxton.* **Scholastic, 2007. 341 p.**
Gr. 5–8. Eleven-year-old Elijah lives with his family in Buxton, Canada, a community of freed slaves. One resident, Mr. Leroy, has been working hard to raise money to free his family. The Preacher, a violent con man, steals the money and heads to America to gamble. Mr. Leroy forces young Elijah to accompany him on the dangerous journey to retrieve the money. Elijah's growing awareness about freedom and slavery is shown through his narrative.

10-Minute Selection: Curtis's remarkable talent for humor is best shown in the second half of chapter 1, "Snakes and Ma." Elijah tricks his mother, playing on her fear of toads. Start reading the sentence, "It waren't but a week later that me and Cooter were down at the river and he yelled, 'Oh, ho . . . !' then snatched a toady-frog big as a pie pan!" Read to the end of the chapter. Elijah hides the toad in his mother's sewing basket. She gets back at him by hiding a little snake in the cookie jar.

Second 10-Minute Selection: Read the entire chapter 11, "Emma Collins and Birdy." Elijah sees strangers hiding in the woods. He finds Pa, and they get Emma Collins. The young girl has a gift of making fearful runaway slaves know that it's all right to enter Buxton and freedom. The reaction of the newcomers as they realize their hard journey is over will make an emotional impact on your listeners.

**Curtis, Christopher Paul.** *Mr. Chickee's Funny Money.* **Wendy Lamb, 2005. 160 p.** Gr. 4–6. Nine-year-old Steven receives a bill worth a quadrillion dollars from his blind, elderly neighbor, Mr. Chickee. Steven's father is convinced the bill is a fake. After all, it has the face of James Brown, the Godfather of Soul, on it. But a trip to the U.S. Treasury Department proves the bill is real, and the government wants it back. A madcap chase ensues that also involves Steven's best friend, Russell, and Russell's dog, Zoopy. The sequel is titled *Mr. Chickee's Messy Mission.*

10-Minute Selection: Read the entire chapter 3, "Getting Closer to the Truth." Steven asks his father what number contains a one with fifteen zeros after it. His father makes Steven work for the answer, including looking in his great-great-grandfather Carter's dictionary, which seemingly talks to Steven in a smart-alecky tone. Continue reading a short, hilarious selection from chapter 4, "Russell and Zippy." Begin with the sentence, "Steven couldn't really complain," and read until Russell's mother's utterance, "The entire family is possessed by Satan, Lord have mercy on their souls." This passage shows how Steven is forced by his father to do and say silly things to rid him of certain bad habits.

**Cushman, Karen.** *Matilda Bone.* **Clarion, 2000. 167 p.** Gr. 5–8. Fourteen-year-old orphan Matilda was raised in a manor. Father Leufredus drops her off at the home of Peg the Bonesetter in the Blood and Bone Alley without explanation. Matilda becomes Peg's assistant. Peg explains that the Blood and Bone Alley is "where ordinary people came to be bled, dosed, and bandaged, with its barber-surgeons down this way and leeches down that." Matilda has trouble adjusting to this new life, clinging to the hope that Father Leufredus will return for her.

10-Minute Selection: Read chapter 13, "Talking to Effie." A woman named Effie is traveling through the village with her husband when she is injured. The highly regarded physician Master Theobald has Effie taken to Peg's shop but does little more than prescribe "a jar of my hare's-foot salve for the cut on her head."

Peg, Matilda, and physician Margery Lewes take over treating Effie. "When Effie's head wound showed signs of putrefaction, Doctor Margery cleaned it with warm wine, placed cobwebs and a pinch of bread mold gently over it, and bound it all together with clean linen." While Effie stays at Peg's to recover, Matilda spends a lot of time talking to her and, in turn, learns a little more about herself.

**Cushman, Karen. *Rodzina*. Clarion, 2003. 203 p.**
Gr. 5–8. Rodzina and several other orphans are on a train heading west from Chicago to find homes. The orphans are accompanied by Mr. Szprot and Miss Doctor, two coldhearted adults. Many of the orphans are worried that they will simply become slaves for their new families. Rodzina successfully talks her way out of one such situation. She also narrowly escapes a man who plans to make twelve-year-old Rodzina his new wife. By the time the train leaves Utah, Rodzina is the only orphan left. "Seemed like I was the most unwanted orphan of all." She and Miss Doctor head for California to enroll Rodzina in a training school. Rodzina comes up with a last-minute idea to salvage her future.

10-Minute Selection: Read chapter 4, "Grand Island." Grand Island, Nebraska, is the first stop for the train. Several people, mostly farmers, line up to look over the orphans. Some are chosen. Rodzina is taken by two old ladies who let it be known that Rodzina will work hard for them. "Can she sew, mend, launder, and iron? . . . Boil ashes and lye for soap? Butcher hogs? Hull, shell, grind, sift, boil, bake, pickle, and pop corn?" As she rides in the wagon on the way to the ladies' farm, Rodzina cleverly convinces them that she will be too much trouble. Miss Doctor and Mr. Szprot are unhappy to see Rodzina return to the train.

**Cutler, Jane. *Leap, Frog*. Farrar Straus Giroux, 2002. 198 p.**
Gr. 2–4. A rambunctious first-grader named Charley moves in next door to brothers Edward and Jason Fraser. Edward helps a couple of seventh-graders decorate their "egg babies" for their health class's "Parenting: Are You Ready?" unit. Charley grabs one of the eggs, and everyone worries that he will break it. Edward has a good idea how Charley's mind works and coaxes him to give up the egg. In another story, Edward and Charley catch a special frog for "The First Annual Mark Twain Memorial Jumping Frog Contest." In the last story, Edward's family invites Charley to attend a local theater production of *The Bremen Town Musicians*. Everyone is stunned and puzzled when Charley kicks an actor in the shins. This is the fourth book about the Fraser boys.

10-Minute Selection: Read the opening chapter, "The New Kid." The dialogue is quite humorous when two sisters try to outdo each other by claiming each one missed the old neighbor the most. Later, Edward witnesses the trick Charley's mother uses to settle down her hyperactive son. Move on to the last half of the chapter titled "Want to Hear Some Frog Jokes?" Start with the sentence, "The boys walked slowly," and read until the end of the chapter. Charley and Edward are heading to the lake to find a frog. They share a lot of frog riddles, such as "What does a frog with long ears say? . . . Rabbit! Rabbit!"

**Delaney, Joseph.** *The Last Apprentice: Revenge of the Witch.* **Greenwillow, 2005. 343 p.**
Gr. 5–10. Thomas is the seventh son of a seventh son. There's no room for him on the farm. His oldest brother inherited it. Thomas is apprenticed to Old Gregory as a Spook. A Spook's job is to deal "with ghouls, boggarts, and all manner of wicked beasties." With little training, Thomas must face the witch Mother Malkin. "She's about as evil as you can get." Thomas is tricked into freeing Mother Malkin from her grave prison. He defeats her once, but she returns and shows up at his family's farm. This is the first book in the series.

10-Minute Selection: Warn your listeners that this is a scary book. Read most of chapter 3, "Number Thirteen Watery Lane." Begin with the line, "Finally we turned a corner into the lowest and meanest street of all," and read to the end of the chapter. The Spook tests young Thomas. "I bring all my new apprentices to this old house on their first night so I can find out what they're made of." Thomas is instructed to go into the cellar at midnight "and face whatever it is that's lurking there." While waiting alone, Thomas hears digging, footsteps, and knocking at the door. He finally heads to the cellar to a big surprise.

**Delaney, Michael.** *Birdbrain Amos.* **Philomel, 2002. 153 p.**
Gr. K–4. A hippopotamus named Amos advertises for a "tick bird" and hires one named Kumba. The two have a slight language barrier. Not only does Kumba eat ticks off of Amos's back but she also builds a nest on his head and lays three eggs. Amos becomes a laughingstock to the other large mammals but doesn't quite know how to handle the situation. The eggs hatch, and one of the birds—Amoeba—remains, even after Kumba leaves. Amos finds himself reluctantly taking care of the little bird. His attitude changes after a python attacks them.

10-Minute Selection: Read chapter 1, "Help Wanted." Amos needs a "tick bird" because "bugs and ticks were crawling all over his body." Amos advertises but fails to mention specifically what type of bird he needs. A thrush that sings Bach and the Beatles applies. Continue reading chapter 2, "The Vulture." Amos finally gets his "tick bird" but only after turning down a vulture that also applied for the job. Finish the selection by reading chapter 3, "Kumba." Amos and Kumba try hard to understand each other's nuances. Amos becomes dismayed when Kumba takes the words "make yourself at home" too literally and builds a nest on top of his head. Be sure to add the funny statement found in the book's front matter: "Resemblances to any hippopotamus, tick birds, or other animal, wild or in captivity, is purely coincidental."

**Denslow, Sharon Phillips.** *Georgie Lee.* **Greenwillow, 2002. 91 p.**
Gr. K–2. J.D. gets to spend the summer on the farm with his grandmother, Georgie Lee the cow, and Boots the cat. J.D. first realizes that Georgie Lee is a smart cow when he watches her wade into a creek. The cow flicks water with her tail across her back, "making any flies there crawl to her belly." The cow then stands so still that little fish gather by her legs. The fish jump up and catch the flies off of Georgie Lee's belly. J.D., Grandmother, and the animals also visit a haunted house, outrun a big storm, catch runaway cows and a bull, and help an elderly neighbor who falls in her orchard.

10-Minute Selection: Read chapter 2, "Up a Tree." J.D. climbs a tree. Boots joins him. Grandmother says, "I used to climb trees," and is soon sitting on a limb next to J.D. When they see the neighbor's cows and bull running down the road, Grandmother realizes, "It seems, J.D., I remember how to climb a tree, but I forgot how to get down." J.D. and Georgie Lee successfully gate the cattle, and then J.D. braves some wasps to get a ladder for Grandmother.

**DiCamillo, Kate.** *Because of Winn-Dixie.* **Candlewick, 2000. 182 p.**
Gr. 3–5. Ten-year-old Opal and her preacher father move to a new town in Florida. Opal misses her mother, who left them, and asks her father to share ten things about her mom. "One thing for each year I've been alive." Opal also finds a stray dog she names Winn-Dixie. The two roam around town and meet an eclectic group of adults and children that includes the town librarian and a pet-shop employee who was once arrested.

10-Minute Selection: Read the first chapter, which begins with one of the best opening lines ever. "My name is India Opal Buloni, and last summer my daddy, the preacher, sent me to the store for a box of macaroni-and-cheese, some white rice, and two tomatoes, and I came back with a dog." The chapter shows how Opal "found" Winn-Dixie. Continue by reading the short chapter 6 and chapter 7. Miss Franny, the librarian, mistakes Winn-Dixie for a bear. She then tells Opal and Winn-Dixie a story about a bear that wandered into the library years ago. "I raised up the book I was reading . . . it was *War and Peace*, a very large book. I raised it up slowly and then I aimed it carefully and I threw it right at the bear and screamed, 'Be gone!' . . . He went. But this is what I will never forget. He took the book with him."

**DiCamillo, Kate.** *The Miraculous Journey of Edward Tulane.* **Candlewick, 2006. 198 p.**
Gr. K–3. Edward Tulane is a china rabbit. His first owner, Abilene, loses him during an ocean cruise, and he is found by a fisherman. The reader follows Edward's travels from owner to owner, including the fisherman's wife, a hobo, a dying girl, and a runaway boy. Edward's china head is eventually smashed by an irate cook

but repaired by a skilled doll maker. Throughout his "miraculous journey," Edward learns about love.

10-Minute Selection: Read chapters 1, 2, and 5. The first chapter introduces Edward to the audience. "He had china arms and china legs, china paws and a china head, a china torso and a china nose. His arms and legs were jointed and joined by wire so that his china elbows and china knees could be bent, giving him much freedom of movement." Chapter 2 shows Edward's irritation at being mishandled by a dog and the new maid. The chapter ends with mention of the ship. Chapter 5 describes how two naughty brothers grab Edward and toss him back and forth. Abilene tackles one of the boys, "upsetting his aim. So it was that Edward did not go flying back into the dirty hands of Martin. Instead, Edward Tulane went overboard."

**DiCamillo, Kate. *The Tale of Despereaux*. Candlewick, 2003. 267 p.**
Gr. 2–5. A tiny mouse named Despereaux finds his life intertwined with Princess Pea, a rat named Roscuro, and Miggery Sow, a servant girl. Despereaux is "the smallest mouse I've ever seen." He has "obscenely large ears" and is sickly. "Most alarming of all, he showed no interest in the things a mouse should show interest in." DiCamillo wrote this story about "an unlikely hero" for a friend. In another part of the castle, Roscuro convinces Miggery to help him kidnap Princess Pea and hide her in the dungeon. Despereaux, who already survived one journey to the dangerous dungeon, attempts to rescue Pea.

10-Minute Selection: Read chapter 10, "Good Reasons." Despereaux is brought before the Mouse Council. He is found guilty of sitting at the foot of the human king and allowing the human princess to touch him. Despereaux faints when he is told that he will be sent to the dungeon for his actions. Move on to the short chapter 14, "Darkness." Despereaux is now in the dark dungeon. "It stank of despair and suffering and hopelessness. Which is to say the dungeon smelled of rats." He tries to be brave. He hears a voice that, "he assumed, belongs to the world's largest rat. . . . And for the second time that day, the mouse fainted."

**Dowd, Siobhan. *The London Eye Mystery*. David Fickling, 2007. 323 p.**
Gr. 5–10. Ted and Kat's cousin Salim boards a sealed pod on the London Eye, Europe's tallest Ferris wheel, but doesn't come off. He simply disappears. Ted, who suffers from Asperger's syndrome, tells us in his own voice how he and his sister develop theories to find out what happened to their cousin. As Ted says, "This is how having a funny brain that runs on a different operating system from other people's helped me figure out what had happened."

10-Minute Selection: Read the first chapter, which gives a brief account of Salim climbing aboard "the largest observation wheel ever built." Ted and Kat track Salim's capsule from the ground but are surprised when Salim doesn't appear. "Somewhere, somehow, in the thirty minutes of riding the Eye, in his sealed capsule, he had vanished off the face of the earth." Move on to the last half of chapter 6, "We Go to the Eye," which covers the incident in more detail. We learn why Salim went up without his cousins. Begin with the sentence, "Then she, Salim and I found the end of the ticket queue and joined it." Read to the end of the chapter and keep on reading the entire chapter 7, "The Wheel Turns." The kids conclude that Salim is gone. "Mum and Auntie Glo are going to be livid."

**Dowell, Frances O'Roark. *Dovey Coe*. Atheneum, 2000. 181 p.**
Gr. 5–8. It's 1928 in rural North Carolina, and twelve-year-old Dovey Coe has been accused of murdering local rich boy Parnell Caraway. Parnell was mad and publicly humiliated when Dovey's older sister, Caroline, turned down his hand in marriage. Dovey's brother, Amos, is deaf; Parnell sends word to Dovey that he has one of Amos's dogs. Dovey slashes her knife at Parnell when he throws a brick at the dog. Dovey is knocked out. When she comes to, she learns that Parnell is dead.

10-Minute Selection: Read the very first page of the book to hook the listeners. The book opens, "My name is Dovey Coe, and I reckon it don't matter if you like me or not. . . . I hated Parnell Caraway as much as the next person, but I didn't kill him." The page ends with "Parnell Caraway was the meanest, vainest, greediest man who ever lived. Seventeen years old and rotten to the core." Move on to chapter 11. Before reading, inform your listeners that Dovey's older sister has just rejected Parnell's hand in marriage. The chapter shows the locals' reactions to this public rejection. Parnell sees Dovey in town and says, "Don't you worry, Dovey Coe. You and me are going to have us a long talk real soon." The passage ends with Dovey alone at her house, watching Parnell's car coming into the yard. "I checked my pocket for my knife. I was figuring I might need to use it."

**Dowell, Frances O'Roark. *Phineas L. MacGuire . . . Erupts! The First Experiment*. Atheneum, 2006. 167 p.**
Gr. 3–5. Fourth-grader Phineas, who is also known as Mac, is upset with the behavior of the new kid, Mac R. The new Mac is very obnoxious. Mrs. Tuttle, their teacher, pairs the two boys for the science fair. Mac learns that Mac R. is a great artist and that his real name is Ben. The refreshing aspect of the story is that Ben is sorry he acted rudely to his classmates, and he wants to rectify the situation. Mac and Ben make an incredibly large volcano to erupt for the science fair. Unfortunately, Ben forgets to bring the vinegar—"No vinegar, no eruption"—and the boys realize the judges are approaching their exhibit. "My scientific career at Woodbrook Elementary School was over." This is the first Phineas L. MacGuire book.

10-Minute Selection: Read the first two chapters. Chapter 1 introduces the listeners to Phineas. He explains why he is called Mac and also states he is allergic to fifteen things, including girls. He also shares his love for science. He misses his best friend, Marcus, who moved away. The two boys "made and erupted over eighty-seven volcanoes in our lifetime." Chapter 2 introduces us to the obnoxious antics of Mac R. that make everyone hate him. Mac R. states that there are no smart girls, which draws the ire of Aretha, "the only person I know who is as excited about the fourth-grade science fair as I am."

**Draper, Sharon M.** *Double Dutch.* **Atheneum, 2002. 183 p.**
Gr. 5–8. Eighth-grader Delia has a secret. She can't read. She's been able to bluff her way through school so far, but if she doesn't pass the state tests, she won't be able to participate in the World Double Dutch Championship. Her friend Randy also has a secret. His father has gone missing, and Randy has been living alone for nearly two months. All the kids at their school are afraid of twin brothers Tabu and Titan Tolliver, who seem likely to attack at any moment. A tornado strikes the school, and the Tollivers, along with Delia's friend Yolanda, go missing.

10-Minute Selection: Read chapter 10. It opens with the kids repeating rumors about the Tollivers. Yolanda runs into the twins and accidentally smears some lipstick on the hand of one of the boys. She sweet-talks her way out of danger, to the amazement of her friends. At a school assembly, the students learn that a metal detector will be set up at the main entrance. Back in class, Miss Benson is asking student groups about their *Lord of the Flies* book project. The Tollivers refuse to give details what they have planned. "'It's gonna be a surprise,' Titan answered. 'You will never forget it.'"

**Dunrea, Olivier.** *Hanne's Quest.* **Philomel, 2006. 95 p.**
Gr. K–4. Mem Pockets is an old woman who lives on a small farm with her dog and several chickens. Hanne, "the youngest, quietest, and the smallest hen," goes on a dangerous journey to help Mem Pockets save her farm. It is said that a hen "who is bravest of heart, purest in thought, and wisest in the ways of the Great Goddess" will be able to lay three golden eggs. An ancient rhyme guides Hanne to an ancient barrow, to the Standing Stones, and finally, to the Great Green Sea. The story has an old-fashioned folklore feel to it. As with many epic literary journeys, "She felt a very different hen than she was when she had first set out from the farm on her quest."

10-Minute Selection: Read chapter 3, where Hanne leaves the farm and goes on her first task. She finds the great barrow, meets a helpful mole, and wanders through a dark tunnel until she encounters the scary barrow-wight, a subterranean creature. The chapter is long. If you'd like to end with a cliff-hanger, finish with the sentence, "Is it getting darker in here? Hanne asked herself," right before she finds the barrow-wight.

**DuPrau, Jeanne.** *Car Trouble.* **Greenwillow, 2005. 274 p.**
Gr. 7–10. Duff, a self-professed geek just out of high school, drives cross-country from Virginia to a high-tech job waiting for him in California. Unfortunately, his car breaks down. He gets an opportunity to drive a different car to St. Louis and deliver it to its owner. The owner turns out to be a swindler who has hidden thousands of ill-gotten dollars in the car. Duff finds himself traveling with a shady character named Stu, an aspiring musician named Bonnie, and her dog, Mooney. Duff's job evaporates even before he reaches California, but he realizes that other things are more important than the job.

10-Minute Selection: Read chapter 6, "The Bikers' Dance." Duff and Stu stop at Pete's Stewpot to grab a bite to eat. The place turns out to be a biker hangout. Duff is forced to dance in front of everyone. "The man with the bandanna was standing over him, scowling. 'Boy,' he said, 'when my lady wants to dance with you, you dance.'" The boys safely make their way out of the place. The chapter ends with Duff realizing his wallet—containing his money, driver's license, and bank cards—is missing. "'I must have left it in that restaurant.' . . . He felt as dark as the night sky. He knew he would never see his wallet again."

**DuPrau, Jeanne.** *The City of Ember.* **Random House, 2003. 270 p.**
Gr. 4–10. Ember is a city of light in a world of darkness. The citizens are worried that the generator that powers the city will fail and plunge them into darkness. Indeed, there are several power outages, a food shortage, and, as the two protagonists—Lina and Doon—discover, corruption in the government. Lina finds a partially destroyed document that may be the instructions to escape Ember. There have been previous attempts to venture into the Unknown Regions, but all have failed. Lina and Doon are branded as troublemakers and flee the populace. In doing so, they discover the true origins of Ember. This is the first book in a series about Ember. Note to the reader: when sections of the document are displayed in the book, don't attempt to read the partial words. Simply mention there are cryptic passages the kids can look at later.

10-Minute Selection: Read chapter 1, "Assignment Day." There is a brief description of Ember. When children turn twelve, they finish school and become workers. On Assignment Day, they meet with their teacher and the mayor and pull postings of available jobs out of a bag. This determines their future. Both Lina and Doon are upset at their assignments. Lina is stuck in one of the worst jobs—Pipeworks laborer—working underground. Doon wants to be an Electrician's helper, but instead he gets Messenger. Lina is overjoyed when Doon swaps with her.

**Dyer, Heather.** *Ibby's Magic Weekend.* **Scholastic, 2008. 144 p.**
Gr. 3–6. A young girl named Ibby spends the weekend with her cousins Francis and Alex. They find a box marked "Magic for Beginners." The children discover that the kit actually produces real magic when Francis shrinks while practicing the "miniaturization" trick. Ibby also tries to solve the mysterious disappearance of Uncle Godfrey, a professional magician who vanished years ago.

10-Minute Selection: Inform your audience that the children in the story have discovered a magic box. Read the list of tricks from the first page of chapter 3. Read chapter 5. Alex learns how to levitate. He ties a rope around his waist. He next asks his cousins to hold on while he goes out the bedroom window. The cousins panic and drop the rope. The chapter ends with the line, "Then, with his arms and legs paddling pathetically, he disappeared beyond the pines." Move to the middle of chapter 10, and start with the sentence, "Francis, meanwhile, was making the most of being invisible." Francis decides to take advantage of this new trick by sneaking into the fair. He rides the Ferris wheel. The workers cannot see him when they shut it down for the evening. Francis is stuck high overhead. End with the line, "Francis huddled in one corner of the seat . . . and for the first time in his life, he knew what it was like to feel truly invisible."

**Elliott, David.** *Evangeline Mudd and the Golden-Haired Apes of the Ikkinasti Jungle.* **Candlewick, 2004. 196 p.**
Gr. 3–5. Evangeline's parents are expert primatologists who study golden-haired apes. They raise Evangeline much in the manner of apes. She's an expert at brachiating—swinging from branch to branch. She's also an exceptional child in most everything she tries. She's sent to live with some awful relatives when her parents head off on a research trip to the dangerous Ikkinasti Jungle. It's up to Evangeline to find her parents when they go missing. The sequel is titled *Evangeline Mudd and the Great Mink Escapade.*

10-Minute Selection: Read chapter 4, "You Tell Her." Evangeline's parents first learn of the opportunity to travel to the Ikkinasti Jungle. Evangeline pleads that she be allowed to go. Her parents warn her of the dangers, such as little wormy things that "enter your bloodstream and turn you the color of a ripe plum," mosquitoes the size of hummingbirds, and the dreaded spitting spiders. If there's time, read chapter 11. Evangeline is vaccinated with twenty or thirty shots but doesn't realize it because of the doctor's hilarious sleight-of-hand tricks. The chapter ends with the doctor telling Evangeline that there is no vaccine for the spitting spiders: "If you run into one of those spitting spiders, you've had it!"

**Erdrich, Louise.** *The Game of Silence.* **HarperCollins, 2005. 248 p.**
Gr. 3–6. Omakayas is an Ojibwa girl who lives on an island on Lake Superior in 1850. She and her people are concerned that the white people, the "chimooko-

manag," will make them move westward, where the Bwaanag, the Dakota and La-kota people, live. "As the chimookomanag push us, so we push the Bwaanag. We are caught between two packs of wolves." We follow a year in the life of Omakayas and other notable characters, such as her pesky brother Pinch, a new boy referred to as the Angry One, a girl named Two Strike who kills a moose and sees herself as a warrior, and Old Tallow, an elderly hunter who lives by herself with her dogs. There are several Ojibwa words; a glossary and pronunciation guide is provided. This is the sequel to Erdrich's book *The Birchbark House.*

10-Minute Selection: Go to chapter 3, "Fish Soup," and read the subsection titled "The Mud People." Omakayas is setting up a play camp with her cousins. Pinch runs through and destroys the girls' play world. He runs up a tree. Two Strike chases him with her hatchet, causing him to fall into muck. "He dripped absurdly, tufts of stinking weed sprouting off his shoulders and hair." Soon, the kids start tossing each other into the mud. End the passage with the line, "Then they chose flat sunny rocks and lay down to dry themselves."

**Fama, Elizabeth. *Overboard.* Cricket, 2002. 158 p.**
Gr. 5–10. Fourteen-year-old Emily lives in Sumatra with her parents, who work for World Physicians for Children. She is on an overcrowded ferry when it sinks in the ocean. Emily spends hours in the water without a life preserver, using her wits to stay alive. She helps a frightened young boy, Isman, who is unable to swim, through a long, dark night. They head for a series of small, deserted islands but are in danger of being swept by strong currents past the islands and into the open sea.

10-Minute Selection: Read the last paragraph of chapter 9, when Emily, who is treading water, is pulled underwater. "She didn't have time to catch a breath. Someone, something was dragging her under from behind. . . . She didn't feel any pain, but she was sure it was a shark." Continue reading the entire chapter 10, where we learn that a woman who doesn't know how to swim is the one pulling Emily down. Emily gets free, and the woman pleads for help before going under again. "Emily froze with fear. The woman was drowning before her eyes. She couldn't just watch; she couldn't let her drown! But Emily was paralyzed."

**Fine, Anne. *The Jamie and Angus Stories.* Candlewick, 2002. 108 p.**
Gr. K–2. A young boy and his toy bull Angus have six different adventures. Angus is accidentally placed in the washing machine and quickly becomes "gray and be-draggled." Nonetheless, Jamie chooses him over a "proud and silky and shiny and new" toy. Other stories find the two attending his babysitter's wedding, spending time in the hospital, and trying to behave like a grown-up for an entire day. The sequel is titled *Jamie and Angus Together.*

10-Minute Selection: Read the first part of chapter 1, which describes how Jamie and Angus came together. Jamie makes a "farm" for Angus out of scraps, cardboard tubes, sponges, mirrors, and Popsicle sticks. He also makes a "stall" out of shoeboxes and corrugated paper. End with the sentence, "He'd waited so long to bury his face in that magnificent silky coat, as smooth as bath water and white as snow." Continue reading the chapter titled "Uncle Edward Teaches Angus to Jump." Uncle Edward is a playful man who takes Jamie upstairs to bedtime. He sits in the bedroom doorway so that he's halfway near Jamie's parents downstairs and "half here with you." While waiting for Jamie to go to sleep, Uncle Edward teaches Angus to do an "amazing, astonishing, wonderful double fancy backward bounce with treble spin and extra twirl."

**Flake, Sharon B.** *Begging for Change.* **Hyperion, 2003. 235 p.**
Gr. 5–12. Raspberry Hill's mother is in the hospital after being attacked by a neighbor girl. Raspberry steals money from her best friend, Zora, before her mother is well enough to return to their apartment. Raspberry also steals from their elderly neighbor. Her father is a homeless drug addict who also steals. She and her mother survive with the help of good friends. Raspberry is ashamed when she learns the money she stole from Zora was to buy a gift for her mother while she was still in the hospital. This is the sequel to Flake's book *Money Hungry.*

　　10-Minute Selection: Read the first chapter. Raspberry is in her mother's hospital room when her father arrives. "All I know is, something stinks real bad. When I lift my head up, there he is. Standing by the door." Next, read chapter 21. Raspberry is alone at her apartment when her father shows up. He has a friend with him. They barge into the apartment and take food. Raspberry catches her father going through her mother's things, and she offers him money. She runs into her bedroom, where she has her special stash. Her father follows. "Daddy's got a hold of my money. Pulling back the rug and taking a whole bunch more. 'That's mine!' I scream. 'I worked for that!'" Her father's friend asks him how much he got, and they head out. "I beg my father again and again not to take my stuff. He looks me right in the eye and says, 'Sorry. But I need this for something.'"

**Funke, Cornelia.** *Igraine the Brave.* **Scholastic, 2007. 224 p.**
Gr. 3–8. Igraine would rather learn to be a knight like her great-grandfather instead of a magician like her parents and brother. Her courage and wit are needed when the evil Osmund lays siege to Igraine's magical castle. Normally, her powerful parents would easily repel an attack, but they mistakenly turned themselves into pigs when a spell went awry. Igraine and her brother find strange allies to help fight Osmund and his henchman, Rowan the Heartless.

　　10-Minute Selection: Read the first half of the opening chapter. We meet Igraine and learn about the cool defensive features of the family castle, including the stone lions, gargoyles, and water snakes. Read up to the line, "I'll bet you ten of your tame mice I'll win the King's tournaments someday." Move on and read the chapter titled "Birthday Breakfast on the Carpet." Igraine receives a magical suit of armor for her birthday. She also learns how her parents turned themselves into pigs. It's up to Igraine to take a dangerous trip to retrieve the giant hairs needed to reverse the spell.

**Funke, Cornelia. *Inkheart*. Scholastic, 2003. 534 p.**
Gr. 4–12. Meggie's father has the ability to bring literary characters into the real world. Unfortunately, while reading a book titled *Inkheart,* he brought the evil Capricorn and his henchmen into the world when Meggie was very young. "Its title is *Inkheart* because it's about a man whose wicked heart is black as ink, filled with darkness and evil." At the same time, Meggie's mother went *into* the book. Other literary characters brought into the world include Farid, from *The Thousand and One Nights;* Tinkerbell, from *Peter Pan;* and Hans Christian Andersen's Steadfast Tin Soldier. When Capricorn learns that Meggie also has the ability to draw characters, he plots to have her bring forth a terrible creature known as the Shadow. This is a great story to read aloud since it is *about* the power of reading aloud. This is the first book in a series.

10-Minute Selection: Read chapter 16, "Once Upon a Time." Mo tells Meggie how Capricorn, Basta, and Dustfinger came into the world. "My voice had brought them slipping out of their story like a bookmark forgotten by some reader between the pages." Capricorn threatened Mo to return him, but Mo didn't know how to control this strange new power. He held Capricorn and Basta off and "they both disappeared into the night, reeling like drunks." That's when Mo realized that his wife was missing. "She went into it, along with our two cats who were curled up on her lap." End the passage with the sentences, "After that I saw no more of him for five years. Until four days ago."

**Gaiman, Neil. *Coraline*. HarperCollins, 2002. 162 p.**
Gr. 4–10. When Coraline's parents go missing, she enters a tiny door in her new house that is usually bricked up. Now, it opens to a tunnel that leads her to a malevolent creature that calls herself Coraline's other mother. Coraline leaves but returns to the strange place after seeing her real parents trapped in a mirror. This time, the other mother traps Coraline. Coraline challenges her other mother; if she can find the lost souls of three ghostly children she met, plus her missing parents, the other mother must let Coraline go free. Coraline rises to the challenge. With the help of a black cat and a mysterious stone, her parents are returned and the three children get their souls back. Unfortunately, the other mother is not quite done with Coraline.

10-Minute Selection: Read the first chapter. It sets up the scenario and throws in a few thrills, too. Coraline's parents don't pay much attention to her. To entertain herself, Coraline explores her new flat and surroundings. She discovers a locked door. Her mother unlocks it, and they find it "didn't go anywhere. It opened onto a brick wall." They neglect to relock it. Later that night, Coraline hears a sound. "Something went kreeee . . . aaaak."

**Gallo, Donald R., ed. *Destination Unexpected.* Candlewick, 2003. 222 p.**
Gr. 7–12. Ten short stories feature teenagers going on journeys, some short, some long. As Gallo says in the introduction, "Arriving at the destination is the goal, certainly, but the experiences during the journey itself are what transform the character." In Joyce Sweeney's "Something Old, Something New," Darius wins a short story contest and leaves his crime-ridden neighborhood on a bus trip to a different part of the city to attend the reception. In Ron Koertge's "Brutal Interlude," Lori makes a big decision about her handsome but goofy boyfriend during a trip to the racetrack. Graham Salisbury's "Mosquito" finds short, sixteen-year-old Ricky trailing after his mother's current boyfriend on a hunting trip because, in the words of his mother, "This is your chance to get out and see something new."

10-Minute Selection: If you had time for only one story in this rich collection, read "Bread on the Water," by David Lubar. Andy and Tommy are kicked out of church for misbehaving. They walk over to a diner, where they treat a homeless man to a meal. They also leave a big tip for the waitress. Afterward, their parents ironically yell at them about their irresponsible behavior.

**Gallo, Donald R., ed. *First Crossing: Stories about Teen Immigrants.***
**Candlewick, 2004. 224 p.**
Gr. 6–12. The title story, written by Pam Muñoz Ryan, follows Marco, who is attempting to cross the border into the United States for the first time. The other stories share emotional immigration experiences of teens and their families from Venezuela, Kazakhstan, China, Romania, Palestine, Sweden, Korea, Haiti, and Cambodia. Contributors include notable young adult writers such as Alden R. Carter, Minfong Ho, David Lubar, Elsa Marston, Lensey Namioka, Jean Davies Okimoto, Dian Curtis Regan, and Rita Williams-Garcia.

10-Minute Selection: Read "Pulling up Stakes," by David Lubar, the most whimsical story from the collection. Adrian and his family travel from Romania to their new home in Alaska. They arrive at a time when the sun is gone for several days. When two classmates hear that Adrian came from the region known as Transylvania, they give him little tests, such as putting extra garlic powder on his pizza, to determine if he's a vampire. He eventually catches on to what they are doing. He's worried that they won't be his friends if they learn he's not a vampire. When everyone in the village gathers to watch the sun rise, he makes an excuse, to the thrill of his friends, to head indoors. Adrian also attracts the attention of a girl named Zinah, who touches the side of her neck and asks, "Do you want to kiss me here?"

**Gantos, Jack.** *Jack Adrift: Fourth Grade without a Clue.* **Farrar Straus Giroux, 2003. 197 p.**
Gr. 4–6. Jack and his family move to Cape Hatteras, North Carolina, when his father rejoins the U.S. Navy. Jack is about to begin fourth grade in a new school and is worried about his new classmates. Jack thinks, "I knew it would be a lot easier to take Dad's advice and just make up something incredible they would think was cool. Or I could simply tell them the truth, the whole truth, and nothing but the truth, which is that I am totally *boring*." Jack develops a crush on his new teacher and works to adapt to his new school and living conditions. This is one of five books about Jack Henry.

10-Minute Selection: Read a section of the chapter titled "The Genius Test." Jack's brother Pete and their young neighbor Julian brag that they are geniuses. The insults fly between the two over who is smarter. Jack referees a series of intellectual challenges. Begin with the sentence, "I just came to let you know that I'm a genius," and proceed through the first two challenges up to the lines, "Okay. Let's just skip the third category."

**Gardner, Lyn.** *Into the Woods.* **David Fickling, 2006. 427 p.**
Gr. 4–8. Three sisters find themselves pursued by the evil Dr. DeWilde and his pack of wolves. Storm and her sisters, Aurora and Anything, must use their wits to survive in an altered-fairy-tale world. They are imprisoned in a house made of sweets, encounter an ogress who turns out to be their great-grandmother, and find themselves in the bowels of a mountain with several enslaved workers. Dr. DeWilde is after a magical pipe that Storm possesses that will bring him great power.

10-Minute Selection: Read the entire chapter 5. The three girls are living on their own when Dr. DeWilde shows up at their house with his lackey, Alderman Snufflebottom. Dr. DeWilde demands the magical pipe and threatens to harm baby Anything. The older girls manage to grab their sister and run outside. The chapter ends with Dr. DeWilde turning to Snufflebottom and saying, "Release the wolves. Just two or three. Enough to let them know I mean business."

**Giff, Patricia Reilly.** *Willow Run.* **Wendy Lamb, 2005. 149 p.**
Gr. 4–7. Meggie and her parents move to Willow Run, Michigan, in 1944. Her father gets a job working in an airplane factory. They left Meggie's German-born grandfather behind in New York. They all worry when Meggie's older brother, Eddie, is reported missing in action. This is a companion to Giff's book *Lily's Crossing*.

10-Minute Selection: Read chapter 1. Meggie catches two older boys painting a red swastika on her grandfather's window. "If this were anywhere else but Rockaway, they'd probably put him in jail. He's got to be a spy." Meggie wipes off the paint with turpentine before her grandfather sees it. Before reading the next section, inform your audience that Meggie and her family moved and had to leave her grandfather behind in New York. Let them also know that Meggie's brother, Eddie, is missing in action. Read chapter 16. The family is worried when a mail truck brings a special delivery. Instead of bad news about Eddie, it's a package from her grandfather. He sent Meggie his "Victory medal from the Great War." He discovered the remains of the painted swastika. "The outline was so faint I might never have seen it. . . . So I send you my Victory medal because what you did was brave. I send it to you so you will be brave when you need to be brave."

**Glatshteyn, Yankev.** *Emil and Karl.* **Roaring Brook, 2006. 194 p.**
Gr. 4–12. The Nazis have just begun to make their presence felt in Austria right before World War II. Two nine-year-old boys have both lost their parents. Emil's parents are taken because they are Jews; Karl's because they are Socialists. The boys stick together and are shuffled from one situation to another. At one point, they are forced to scrub pavement with several adults. A strange woman leads the boys to a house on the outskirts of town. They learn that this woman, Aunt Matilda, and Uncle Hans, who they think is an idiot, are part of a resistance. The boys are on their own again when a traitor turns the older couple over to the Nazis. The boys vow to remain friends together always but are finally separated at a train station. The novel was originally written in Yiddish in 1940 and is considered one of the first novels for young people to describe what faced the Jewish people in Europe.

10-Minute Selection: Read chapter 2. Karl recalls an incident at school when his beloved teacher joins her students spitting at and taunting Emil. The teacher later confesses to Karl that she doesn't have the strength to fight what is happening. She asks for him to be merciful when he and others make judgment on her. Her attitude changes in a split second as the other students burst in. "You swine . . . you must understand the difference between yourself and the Jews."

**Graff, Nancy Price.** *Taking Wing.* **Clarion, 2005. 211 p.**
Gr. 4–8. Thirteen-year-old Gus is living on his grandparents' Vermont farm because his father is a pilot serving in World War II and his mother is ill. When his grandfather accidentally kills a mother duck, Gus volunteers to raise the duck's eggs. His grandfather asks him, "'Are you ready?' 'Ready for what?' Gus asked, suddenly afraid that something terrible happened in the night. 'To be a mother,' his grandfather said." The task turns out to be difficult, as not all of the eggs hatch ducklings and not all of the ducklings survive.

10-Minute Selection: Read the middle section of chapter 2. Begin with the sentence, "Ten days after Gus's grandfather had set up the incubator, Gus was growing discouraged." Gus startles a girl who is poking around the barn looking at the eggs. She drops one of the eggs. This is the first time we meet Louise Lavictoire, who quickly becomes Gus's friend. Louise's family is from Canada and faces prejudice from the locals, including Gus's grandparents. End the passage when Grandmother says, "The first time you catch her stealing something will be the last time she'll be welcome here."

**Grant, Michael.** *Gone.* **HarperCollins, 2008. 558 p.**
Gr. 6–12. Every adult in the area surrounding Perdido Beach vanishes. Television, radio, and the Internet stop working. Children are left to fend for themselves. And then, even weirder things happen. Some children develop strange powers. Some animals start mutating. Several bullies start to take over what's left of the community. The remaining children learn that once they turn fifteen, they vanish, just like the adults. This apocalyptic book has some elements of *The Stand,* by Stephen King, and *The Lord of the Flies,* by William Golding.

10-Minute Selection: Read the opening chapter. Listeners will be immediately hooked when they hear the opening lines. "One minute the teacher was talking about the Civil War. And the next minute he was gone. There. Gone." Sam and the other students run through the school looking for any adult. They try calling 911 and learn the phones aren't working. We also learn a little about Sam, who earned the nickname School Bus Sam. A few years earlier, he saved a busload of kids when the driver suffered a heart attack. The chapter ends with the cryptic passage, "Life in Perdido Beach had changed. Something big and terrible had happened. Sam hoped he was not the cause."

**Griffin, Adele.** *My Almost Epic Summer.* **Putnam, 2006. 170 p.**
Gr. 6–8. Fourteen-year-old Irene is fired from her hairstyling job by her mother, who is actually the salon owner, and is forced to take a summerlong babysitting job. "Lainie and Evan aren't the worst kids in the world, but I couldn't imagine dealing with them regularly. Babysitting is a job that usually requires at least one day recovery time." Irene meets Starla, a lifeguard with an attitude, and gets sucked into Starla's little world.

10-Minute Selection: Read the chapter titled "Lainie Astonishes Me." Irene plays the game Food Chicken with her young charges, Lainie and Evan. The three add different food items to a mixing bowl and have to take bites of the concoctions as bets. The person who eats the last concoction wins the game and all of the money. (The younger kids kick in their allowances.) The first batch has the three adding raisins, dry oats, and horseradish, which all three eat with little problem. Other combinations include frozen peas–baking powder–soy sauce and farmer's chutney–leftover macaroni and cheese–raw egg. The final mixture is Christmas fruitcake and dog food.

**Grimes, Nikki.** *Bronx Masquerade.* **Dial, 2002. 167 p.**
Gr. 7–12. The members of a diverse high school class establish Open Mike Friday to read their original poetry and reveal their inner selves at the same time. The

students in Mr. Ward's class slowly learn a lot more about each other through the poems. Chankara writes about physical violence. Raul expresses ethnic pride. Devon tells people to look beyond his athletic ability. Gloria shares what it's like to be a teenage mother. The book is set up so that every student shares their thoughts before reading their poems. One of the students, Tyrone, then comments on each student and his or her poem. Tyrone sums up the experience at an all-school assembly. "I'm really glad I got to do this poetry thing because I feel like, even though the people in our class are all different colors and some of you speak a different language and everything, I feel like we connected." The book contains a few Spanish phrases.

10-Minute Selection: Read Gloria Martinez's entry. Gloria struggles with attending school and dreaming of college because she also has to take care of her infant son. Her poem, "Message to a Friend," lets her classmates know how her life changed when "she stopped / caught the toothless, squirming bundle / heaven dropped into her arms / and gravity kicked in."

**Haddix, Margaret Peterson. *Found.* Simon and Schuster, 2008. 314 p.**
Gr. 4–10. A mysterious airplane shows up with nobody aboard except for thirty-six babies. Thirteen years later, Jonah receives a mysterious letter that says, "You are one of the missing." Jonah and his friend Chip are adopted. They learn the warning has something to do with their true identities. The two boys and Jonah's sister, Katherine, begin an investigation that involves the FBI and two opposing factions who have traveled from the future.

10-Minute Selection: Read the prologue. It is Angela DuPre's first day on the job for Sky Trails Air. She looks at Gate 2B and sees a plane appear out of thin air. Nobody is in the cockpit. She ventures down the ramp and sees an open jet door. She steps aboard and finds "thirty-six seats on this plane, and every single one of them was full. Each seat contained a baby." Next, tell your audience that two adopted children, Jonah and Chip, and Jonah's sister, Katherine, have found some mysterious files from the FBI. One of the files has the name Angela DuPre, the woman from the prologue. Then read chapter 13. The children make plans to meet Angela, who is very secretive, at the public library. There's a brief humorous section where Angela quickly spots the kids' efforts to spy on her. When Chip asks Angela if she knows where he came from, she shakes her head no. "'Not where, exactly,' she said apologetically. 'But I think I might have a pretty good guess about when.'"

**Haddix, Margaret Peterson. *Say What?* Simon and Schuster, 2004. 91 p.**
Gr. 1–4. Sukie notices her parents are acting weird. When she gets into trouble, her mother and father respond by saying inappropriate clichés. She runs with a container of glitter in the living room, something her parents had forbidden her

to do. Her father catches her and responds with, "If all your friends jumped off a bridge, would you jump off a bridge too?" Surprised, she drops the glitter on the carpet and her father says, "Don't pick your nose. That's a gross habit." Sukie and her brothers call for an all-kid meeting. The children eventually learn that their parents are experimenting with a new child-rearing theory that they saw in a magazine. In the end, the entire family draws up a list of rules they all could live with.

10-Minute Selection: Read chapter 5. It basically reviews the parents' strange behavior from the previous four chapters. The children decide that they are going to purposely misbehave and study their parents' responses. "We've got to be bad. On purpose." Move on to chapter 7. The children have their second all-kid meeting. They spent the entire day being naughty, but their parents continued to respond with inappropriate phrases. The kids worry that their parents are really robots, "or maybe our real mom and dad have been kidnapped by aliens and the aliens replaced them with fakes that look just like our real mom and dad."

**Hale, Bruce. *The Possum Always Rings Twice*. Harcourt, 2006. 112 p.**
Gr. 1–4. Chet Gecko is a lizard sleuth who attends Emerson Hicky Elementary School with other species of animals. There's a school election, and candidates are receiving anonymous threats to drop out of the race. Chet tries to solve the mystery while dodging bullies and, unsuccessfully, avoiding detention. The book is full of detective-movie-inspired lingo ("That whole thing was fishier than the bottom of a pelican's lunch box") as well as wisecracks that are a delight to read aloud ("I discovered that politicians and diapers should be changed regularly"). There are several puns that might fly over the heads of the intended audience, but the adults will enjoy reading about Ben Dova the wolverine, Viola Fuss the sandpiper, and Natalie Attired the mockingbird. This is one of many Chet Gecko mysteries.

10-Minute Selection: Start with the opening chapter, "The Boy Who Cried Wolverine." The wisecracking Chet is chased by two bullies: Ben Dova, and Miss Flappy the bat. Move on to chapter 11, "Campaign and Caviar." Chet has been convinced to run for election. He goes wild making campaign promises he'll never be able to keep, such as getting rid of history and math. "'We'll get back to the basics,' I said, 'like comic book reading, and ultimate Frisbee, and bungee jumping.'"

**Hale, Shannon. *The Goose Girl*. Bloomsbury, 2003. 383 p.**
Gr. 5–8. Princess Ani is traveling to another kingdom to wed a prince when her guards are killed. The murderers are intent on delivering a false princess in her place. She escapes and eventually arrives at the new kingdom. She finds employment as a goose girl, tending a flock of geese while hiding from her foes. Ani has

the natural ability to speak to some birds and animals and eventually learns she can also speak to the wind. As a goose girl, she learns more about the kingdom than she would have from the palace. Her identity is discovered, and her life is once more in danger.

10-Minute Selection: Beforehand, explain to your audience that Princess Ani is traveling with a company to a new kingdom to get married to a prince she has never met. She has the ability to communicate with Falada, her horse. Read the last section of chapter 4, beginning with the sentence, "A week after the waterfall, the company came to a tree as thick as five men that had fallen across the end," and read to the end of the chapter. Ani learns of the betrayal. There is a fight, and Ani flees into the forest.

**Hale, Shannon. *Princess Academy*. Bloomsbury, 2005. 314 p.**
Gr. 4–8. Miri and the other residents on Mount Eskel quarry linder, a precious and somewhat magical stone. Miri and nineteen other girls on the mountain have been chosen to attend a princess academy partway down the mountain. Prophets have foreseen that the young heir to the kingdom, who resides in the lowlands, will marry a Mount Eskel girl. The young women miss their families, but many are excited at the thought of becoming the future queen. First, the girls have to endure their no-nonsense teacher, Tutor Olana. While the girls wait for the prince's decision, they are first snowed in and then kidnapped by murderous bandits. Miri learns how to use the mountain's magic to call for help.

10-Minute Selection: Read chapter 4. Olana strikes Miri as punishment for speaking out of turn. Miri is again punished for speaking out, which results in a group punishment. "'None of you will be returning to your families tomorrow,' said Olana. 'You will spend the rest of the day in personal study.'" Olana also insults the girls. "Your brains are naturally smaller, I've heard. Perhaps due to the thin mountain air?" This makes Miri determined. "She was going to show Olana that she was as smart as any Danlander. She was going to be academy princess."

**Harkrader, L. D. *Airball: My Life in Briefs*. Roaring Brook, 2005. 198 p.**
Gr. 4–8. Kirby doesn't consider himself a good-enough player to be on his small town's seventh-grade basketball team. However, he tries out because he learns that his team will be meeting hometown hero Brett "McNet" McGrew, who is retiring from the NBA. Kirby becomes convinced that Brett McGrew is really his father. Kirby and his teammates' basketball skills are pretty awful. Their coach comes up with a new strategy that actually works—the boys must play their games in their underwear.

10-Minute Selection: Read chapter 3, where we learn about the legendary Brett McNet and the impact he had on the small town. "Folks around here claim Brett McGrew could dribble before he could walk." Kirby also tells his best friend,

Bragger, about his theory that the basketball star is indeed his father. Skip to the very short chapter 6, where Kirby's grandmother bakes a huge black and orange meatloaf in the shape of a basketball. "What Grandma's meals lack in flavor and chewability, they make up for in sheer volume."

**Hautman, Peter. *Rash*. Simon and Schuster, 2006. 249 p.**
Gr. 6–12. Bo is sentenced to three years at a prison facility near Hudson Bay because he *almost* hit another boy. He had three previous strikes: hitting a kid with a pencil, shoving another kid against a wall, and verbally attacking his rival, Karlohs. It's the end of the twenty-first century, and the USSA (yes, they added an *S*) passed the "Child Safety Act" back in 2033 to extend life. Alcohol and body piercing are illegal, pizza is considered an old person's food choice, and McDonald's is the number-one employer in the nation. Their main business went from selling fast food "back when French Fries were legal" to maintaining prisons. Football has also been banned, except at the prison Bo has been sent to. Shortly after his arrival, Bo finds himself on the prison football team, led by a psychotic coach named Hammer. The book contains a few mild swear words that can be edited out or read.

10-Minute Selection: Read chapter 19. Bo is arriving at the prison. He quickly learns that polar bears surround the facility. "Something happens to one of you—and things do happen here—we just toss you over the fence. Attempted escape." This passage also gives a little background of historical events in the late twenty-first century. "Ever since the USSA annexed Canada during the Diplomatic Wars of 2055 . . ."

**Hautman, Peter, and Mary Logue. *Snatched*. Putnam, 2006. 176 p.**
Gr. 7–10. Two high school students—Roni, a school reporter, and Brian, a troublemaker—set out to investigate the disappearance of popular student Alicia. The opening line, "Alicia watched the blood drip from her nose to the grass," will catch the attention of your listeners. The brief chapters help make the story flow at a fast pace. Roni and Brian find several suspects. Their own lives are at risk as they seek to find the truth. This is the first book in the Bloodwater Mysteries series.

10-Minute Selection: Read the first four very short chapters. Chapter 1, "Poison Honey," finds Alicia in trouble. Chapter 2, "Girl Talk," shows Roni trying to interview Alicia about the attack. Roni's persistence leads her to tackle Alicia. In chapter 3, "Suspended," Roni is told that she is facing a mandatory four-day suspension from school for fighting. Chapter 4, "The Stench," finds Brian in the office with Roni. This meeting of the two leads to the investigation when Alicia goes missing later in the story. The chapter ends as Brian's science-experiment prank fills the school with a stench that smells like "an invisible wave of rotten eggs, ancient sewage, and a dead skunk."

**Heneghan, James.** *Payback.* **Groundwood, 2007. 184 p.**
Gr. 6–10. Charley Callaghan is a new immigrant, having just moved from Ireland to Vancouver. He's dealing with his mother's recent death and bullies at his school. He starts the book with the line, "This story is not about me. It's about a boy named Benny Mason." Despite this statement, the book is definitely about Charley. He's relieved when the bullies start picking on Benny but feels guilty when he doesn't come to Benny's aid. Tragedy strikes, and Charley's guilt grows. The book is split into two sections: part 1 is "Before," and part 2 is "After." Charley's voice is instrumental in both sections as we see how he copes before and after the tragic incident.

10-Minute Selection: Start partway into the first chapter with the sentence, "So now in the schoolyard, Sammy and Rebar, having heard me read aloud, are in my face." Continue to the end of the chapter. Charley tries to put up a fierce front with the bullies, but they just laugh at him. Read the entire third chapter, where we—along with Charley and the bullies—meet the new student, Benny Mason. Sammy and Rebar immediately target Benny. Charley thinks, "I feel sorry for him, but it's his own fault if he won't stand up to them." End the passage with the last section of chapter 10, starting with the line, "I've got the damaged Socials textbook in my room at Aunt Maeve's." Charley reads the famous quote, attributed to Martin Niemöller, that begins "In Germany they came first for the communists and I didn't speak up because I'm not a communist . . ."

**Hiaasen, Carl.** *Flush.* **Knopf, 2005. 263 p.**
Gr. 4–8. Noah's father is in jail for sinking a casino boat near the Florida Keys because he believes the boat is dumping human waste into the water. Noah and his sister, Abbey, try to prove the boat is indeed engaged in illegal activities. They are also trying to prevent their mother from divorcing their eccentric father. An odd assortment of characters helps the kids in this fast-paced eco-mystery.

10-Minute Selection: Read the opening passage of the book, where Noah visits his father in jail. Stop at the line, "I believe you are, Noah," and pick up a few pages later with the sentence, "The Coral Queen had gone down stern-first in twelve feet of water." This gives the audience a good sense of what the father did to the boat. Move on and read the first half of chapter 4. While fishing, Noah encounters the son of the casino owner, Jasper Jr., who promptly punches Noah in the eye. Noah gets even when he makes an incredible cast and hooks Jasper as he's leaving in a motorboat. Jasper's friend Bull tries to cut the line, but their combined weight at the back of the boat causes it to sink. End with the line, "So I reeled in my line and made my way up the slope, toward the highway."

**Hiaasen, Carl.** *Hoot.* **Knopf, 2002. 292 p.**
Gr. 4–8. Roy is new to Florida. He soon gets caught up in a controversy concerning a new pancake house that's being built on a plot that is home to burrowing owls. The company denies the owls exist. "'What's gonna happen to them?' Officer Delinko asked. 'Once you start bulldozing, I mean.' Curly the foreman chuckled. He thought the policeman must be kidding. 'What owls?' he said." Someone is vandalizing the construction site by pulling stakes, slashing tires, and sticking alligators in the portable latrines. "Curly was flabbergasted. 'Are they . . . big gators?' Officer Delinko shrugged, nodding toward the Travelin' Johnnys. 'I imagine all of 'em look big,' he said, 'when they're swimming under your butt.'"

10-Minute Selection: Read the first few pages of chapter 1. While being harassed by Dana the bully, Roy spots a mysterious boy out the school-bus window. End with the sentence, "For a moment he wondered if he'd really seen it himself." Continue reading the entire second chapter. Roy gets into trouble when he breaks Dana's nose while being strangled by Dana. "The punch landed on something moist and rubbery." He also crosses a strong girl who warns him to mind his own business in regard to the mysterious running boy.

**Higgins, F. E.** *The Black Book of Secrets.* **Feiwel and Friends, 2007. 273 p.**
Gr. 5–10. Young Ludlow Fitch escapes from his cruel parents and finds himself apprenticed to Joe Zabbidou, a pawnbroker of secrets. The two set up shop in the isolated mountain village of Pagus Parvus, which is under the sway of the evil Jeremiah Rachet. Joe and Ludlow gain the trust of the villagers, who, one by one, sell their darkest secrets to the pawnbroker. It is Ludlow's job to record the secrets in *The Black Book of Secrets.* As Rachet loses his control over the villagers, he becomes more dangerous to the pawnbroker.

10-Minute Selection: Read the exciting opening chapter, which wastes no time in hooking the reader. Ludlow's evil parents, consumed with the love of alcohol, have bound their son so that "the notorious tooth surgeon of Old Goat's Alley," Barton Gumbroot, can extract Ludlow's teeth and resell them to rich people. Move on to chapter 12, "The Gravedigger's Confession." Tell your audience that Ludlow has joined up with a mysterious pawnbroker who buys people's secrets. Obadiah Strang is the local gravedigger. He has fallen "afoul of my landlord Jeremiah Rachet," who then makes Obadiah do horrible tasks.

**Hill, Kirkpatrick.** *The Year of Miss Agnes.* **Margaret K. McElderry, 2000. 113 p.**
Gr. 3–5. Ten-year-old Fred, short for Frederika, chronicles the 1948 school year, the year Miss Agnes spent teaching in an Alaskan Athabascan village. Miss Agnes is the first instructor to inspire her students to dream great things for their futures.

She throws out the old textbooks and writes personalized books for each student. However, Miss Agnes is homesick for her homeland, England. She informs the kids that she, like most of the teachers that preceded her, will be in their one-room school for only one year.

10-Minute Selection: Reach the short chapter 1. An unnamed teacher bolts for the mail plane, yelling, "Please. Take me back to town. I can't stay in this place another second." The pilot returns a short time later with the new teacher. "This one's got a little mileage. You kids are not going to get away with nothin'." Continue with chapter 8. Miss Agnes spots Bokko for the first time. Bokko is Fred's deaf sister. None of the previous teachers wanted to teach Bokko. Miss Agnes convinces the girls' mother to send Bokko to school. Soon, everyone is learning sign language.

**Hobbs, Will.** *Wild Man Island.* **HarperCollins, 2002. 179 p.**
Gr. 4–10. Fourteen-year-old Andy takes his kayak and leaves his wilderness group in the middle of the night to visit the spot his archaeologist father perished years before. He gets caught in a storm and barely makes it to Admiralty Island, off the Alaskan coast. He is cold and wet. He has no matches or food. There are bears and wolves on the island. A Newfoundland dog is running with the wolves. Andy finds old, abandoned buildings. While exploring them, he is startled to hear footsteps. A tall man with a full gray beard, carrying a spear, is also on the island. As the story progresses, Andy finds the man's hideout as well as significant archaeological finds.

10-Minute Selection: Read chapter 5. Andy has just crawled from the ocean onto a beach. He staggers about, looking for shelter from the rain. He finds a downed tree and crawls into "a burrow in the underside of the rotten log" to get warm. Eventually, he makes plans to return to the beach to locate his kayak and watch for rescue planes "when a bit of motion caught my eye. Something was coming down through the forest." The passage ends on the next paragraph. "It was a bear as big as a haystack, with a wide face and a prominent hump behind its shoulders."

**Horvath, Polly.** *The Pepins and Their Problems.* **Farrar Straus Giroux, 2004. 179 p.**
Gr. 2–6. The Pepins are an unusual family. They simply cannot think of practical solutions to solve their problems. One problem concerns the fact that their cow gives lemonade instead of milk. Another dilemma focuses on how one reheats hot chocolate when it has gone cold. The narrator-author invites the readers to send their solutions to the Pepins' problems directly to her. "Fortunately, this author is endowed with unusually large psychic antennae. She is deeply attuned to her readers. If you put one finger on each temple and concentrate, she will be able to hear your solution and share it with the Pepins and other readers."

10-Minute Selection: Read the first chapter, "Toads in Their Shoes." The Pepin family members learn, with the help of readers, why their shoes are filled with toads. After solving that problem, they climb a ladder up to their roof. The ladder falls and they are trapped. Continue reading the next chapter, "Grilled Lemonade Sandwiches, Anyone?" Neighbors assemble on the ground below offering solutions. None of these solutions include the practical idea of placing the ladder against the house again. End the selection with the passage, "It was not a spectacular descent. 'But,' said Mrs. Pepin as she later related the story to a party of hat-wearing tea drinkers, 'we were all a bit tired by then.'"

**Hunter, Erin. *Warriors: Into the Wild*. HarperCollins, 2003. 272 p.**
Gr. 4–8. Four clans of wild cats have coexisted in the wilderness. This allegiance is threatened when a new leader takes over the ShadowClan. Rusty, a domestic cat, also known as "a kittypet," ventures into the woods and successfully fights a wild cat. Rusty is invited to join the ThunderClan, led by Bluestar. Rusty learns how to be a warrior under Bluestar's guidance. This is the first book in the popular Warriors series.

10-Minute Selection: Read most of chapter 3. Begin with the sentence, "Rusty found himself enjoying the morning even more than usual, visiting his old haunts with Smudge, sharing words with the cats he had grown up with." Rusty is led to the ThunderClan camp for the first time. Many of the wild cats look at him with suspicion and contempt. A tabby named Longtail challenges Rusty, and the two cats fight. Longtail gains the advantage as Rusty is being choked by his own collar. Rusty wins the battle and becomes known as Firepaw.

**Jenkins, Emily. *Toys Go Out*. Schwartz and Wade, 2006. 117 p.**
Gr. K–2. Six stories follow the adventures of a little girl's toys. Stingray is a cloth toy that spouts facts that are anything but accurate. Lumphy is a toy buffalo, and Plastic is a bouncing ball. The first story finds the toys packed together in a backpack. Stingray guesses, among other places, that they are going to the vet, the zoo, and the garbage dump. "It will be icy cold all the time, and full of garbage-eating sharks, and it will smell like throw-up." They find themselves the center of attention at their girl's classroom's show-and-tell. Other highlights include Plastic going to the beach and getting caught by a "possible shark" (a dog) and Lumphy trying to snuggle in bed with the girl and Stingray but not being able to fall asleep. These stories are reminiscent of A. A. Milne's Winnie the Pooh stories.

10-Minute Selection: Read chapter 3, "The Terrifying Bigness of the Washing Machine." Lumphy gets peanut butter smeared on him. He hears the girl's father say, "Lumphy will have to be washed." Stingray goes on and on about the dark, dirty basement, so Lumphy hides. The girl eventually finds him, and Lumphy meets the washing machine, named Frank. After his initial trip through the wash cycle, Lumphy goes out of his way to get dirty and visit Frank again.

**Johnson, Angela.** *Bird.* **Dial, 2004. 132 p.**
Gr. 5–10. Thirteen-year-old runaway Bird hides out in a farmhouse shed. She is looking for her stepfather, who left Bird and her mother a few years earlier. Ethan, a recent heart-transplant recipient, befriends Bird. The two of them tell the story along with Jay, whose brother, Derek, recently passed away. Derek's heart is now inside of Ethan. We meet other characters who have links to all three youngsters. Young audience members won't have any trouble following as the story shifts among the three narrators.

10-Minute Selection: Read the opening chapter, which shows Bird hiding and spying on a farm family. Bird knows their routines. When the family goes to church, Bird breaks into their home, eats their food, and takes a bath.

Second 10-Minute Selection: Read chapter 3. Jay talks about missing his brother. He and his friend Googy steal a pickup truck and go joyriding. He can't stop thinking about Ethan, who carries his brother's heart. "Maybe his heart is searching for and not finding the place it used to live. I understand that because mine is searching and not finding too."

**Jonell, Lynne.** *Emmy and the Incredible Shrinking Rat.* **Holt, 2007. 352 p.**
Gr. 3–5. Emmy discovers she can talk to the classroom pet rat, Raston, in this Dahl-like animal fantasy. This ability is a direct result of being bitten by Raston. Emmy soon learns that a second bite by the rat causes a human to shrink, and a third bite causes the strangest reaction yet. Emmy finds more caged rodents, each with a different power. The evil nanny Miss Barmy is also aware of the rodents' strange abilities. The sequel is titled *Emmy and the Home for Troubled Girls.*

10-Minute Selection: Read chapter 6. Emmy has rescued the rat from his cage but has now returned to school with the rat hiding in her backpack. Professor Vole, who is working in conjunction with Miss Barmy, enters the classroom. He makes up a story about losing the rat years ago. Emmy's teacher is ready to hand the rat over when they notice he's not in his cage. "Emmy heard a sound like a snarling dog. Only it wasn't a dog at all. It was the rat man, and he was looking straight at her." Continue reading the first part of the next chapter, where Emmy's teacher shows some backbone and forces Professor Vole to leave. End with the sentence, "The Rat, in his terror, had peed."

**Kerrin, Jessica Scott.** *Martin Bridge: Ready for Takeoff!* **Kids Can, 2005. 120 p.**
Gr. K–4. Martin learns valuable life lessons in a trio of stories. One story finds Martin taking care of his little neighbor's hamster, Ginny. He's distraught when he finds that Ginny has died. Martin is disturbed that his friend's mother asks him to buy an identical hamster and pretend that it's Ginny. "Once the purchase was made, the store clerk asked, 'What will you name her?' 'Fake-o Ginny,' said Martin bitterly." Martin fights with his good friend Alex in another story. Martin

accuses Alex of stealing his idea and then not giving him proper credit. This is the first book in a series about Martin Bridge.

10-Minute Selection: Read the first chapter, "Riddles." Martin's mean bus driver, Mrs. Phips, is in the hospital. The new driver, Jenny, shares riddles with the kids and remembers their names. "Mrs. Phips never remembered anyone's name. Mostly she'd yell, 'You kids!' as in 'You kids better keep it down back there!'" Martin and the kids decorate the bus with tissue paper and a sign that reads "World's Best Driver." They are surprised to see Mrs. Phips has returned. The former, cranky driver is touched, however, when she thinks the kids decorated the bus for her.

**Key, Watt. *Alabama Moon*. Farrar Straus Giroux, 2006. 294 p.**
Gr. 5–8. Ten-year-old Moon Blake has always lived off the land. His father was an antigovernment loner who shunned people. When his father dies, Moon finds himself trapped in a boys' home. He escapes with some other boys and heads back to the woods. The other boys have romantic notions about living off the land, but reality quickly dashes those notions. Moon, however, is in his element. A mean constable has it in for Moon and pursues them. Some minor editing might be necessary because of salty language. This shouldn't prevent a young audience from getting caught up in this fast-paced adventure story.

10-Minute Selection: Read chapter 19. Moon and two other boys from the home are hiding in the woods. They hear a bloodhound, and Moon prepares to fight it. Read the next chapter. Moon befriends the dog, which decides to join the boys. Skip ahead and read a brief, humorous section of chapter 22 to show the same thing happening with a second dog. Start at the line, "Sanders is back with another dog," and continue to the sentence, "What're we going to do with all these damn dogs?"

**King-Smith, Dick. *Lady Lollipop*. Candlewick, 2000. 122 p.**
Gr. K–4. Princess Penelope is a terribly spoiled child. In fact, everyone agrees that she "was a right pain in the neck." For her eighth birthday, she demands that her father, the king, get her a pig. Penelope receives a very skinny pig, along with the pig's owner, Johnny. Johnny stays on because the pig will not respond to Penelope's commands. Lollipop the pig is very intelligent. She and Johnny earn a special place in the kingdom. Their secret mission is to make Princess Penelope less selfish. The sequel is titled *Clever Lollipop*.

10-Minute Selection: Read the first two chapters. We meet Princess Penelope and witness her terrible tantrums. "I wanna pig, I wanna pig, I wanna pig!" We see her select Lollipop out of all the best pigs in the kingdom. Lollipop proves her intelligence by sitting and rolling over, but she'll only listen to Johnny's commands. Johnny becomes Penelope's personal pig keeper. Continue reading a few pages into the third chapter. Finish with the passage where Johnny says this about Princess Penelope: "'I've been quite successful at training you,' Johnny Skinner said to the pig. 'I wonder if I could train her?'"

**Korman, Gordon. *Island: Book One; Shipwreck.* Scholastic, 2001. 129 p.**
Gr. 3–6. Six kids—four boys and two girls—have been sent to participate in the "Charting a New Course" program. The kids have either been in trouble with the law or have been sent by their parents to change their behavior. They find themselves working as part of the crew on the *Phoenix* in the middle of the Pacific Ocean. One of the kids panics during a storm, leading to a series of events that eventually sinks the boat. An explosion throws all the kids into the water. Four of them huddle together on a makeshift raft; the other two are missing. This is the first book in the Island series. The story ends with the kids landing on an island and will leave your listeners demanding the next book.

10-Minute Selection: Read chapter 9. A storm approaches. J.J., a rich, spoiled kid, goes against the captain's orders and raises the sails. "It was as if the whole world suddenly tilted ninety degrees. The sixty-foot boat was blown all the way over on its side." The chapter ends with the captain pitched overboard. Continue with chapter 10. The engine fails to start, and the wind and waves push the boat further from the spot the captain went in. Eventually, the wind subsides. "When Mr. Radford ordered them all to bed, nobody asked about the captain. They already knew."

**Korman, Gordon. *No More Dead Dogs.* Hyperion, 2000. 180 p.**
Gr. 5–8. This lighthearted, improbable comedy features Wallace Wallace, a local football hero, whose sharp tongue leads to a school suspension. Wallace's less-than-favorable assessment of his English teacher's favorite book, *Old Shep, My Pal*, earns him detention until he turns in another report. The teacher is also directing a play adapted from *Old Shep* and forces Wallace to attend rehearsals. Surprisingly, Wallace makes suggestions for improving the play and becomes a local hero in a different way.

10-Minute Selection: Read the first chapter. We learn why Wallace feels compelled to tell the truth. By doing so, he alienates some people. When asked his opinion about a neighbor's cake, he replies, "It tastes like vacuum cleaner fuzz." He also informs Mr. Fogelman, his English teacher, that *Old Shep, My Pal* was too predictable. He knew the dog was going to die, "Because the dog always dies. Go to the library and pick out a book with an award sticker and a dog on the cover. Trust me, that dog is going down." Move on to the next entry, "Enter . . . Rachel Turner." Begin with the sentence, "Wallace pulled a few sheets of paper from his backpack, and handed them to the director." Wallace complains that the book's dialogue isn't realistic: "I know for a fact that I've never said anything as stupid as, 'Great heavens, this dog has suffered an injury!'" Read until the sentence, "'That's enough rewriting for one day,' Mr. Fogelman decided."

**Landy, Derek.** *Skulduggery Pleasant.* **HarperCollins, 2007. 392 p.**
Gr. 5–10. Twelve-year-old Stephanie's rich, eccentric uncle dies, leaving her his fortune. He also leaves a lot of trouble and a hint of Stephanie's true nature. Uncle Gordon dabbled in magic and had a key that leads to the Scepter, a device that allows its owner the power to rule the world. Stephanie, later named Valkyrie Cain, meets a detective known as Skulduggery Pleasant. Skulduggery is, in fact, a living, walking skeleton and a friend of her uncle. Soon, vampires, the Hollow Men, the White Cleaver, and something known simply as a monster attack Stephanie. "'That, my dear Valkyrie, is what we call a monster.' She looked at Skulduggery. 'You don't know what it is, do you?' 'I told you before what it is, it's a horrible monster. Now shut up before it comes over here and eats us.'" The sequel is titled *Playing with Fire.*

   10-Minute Selection: Read the last section of chapter 2, "The Will." Begin with the sentence, "Can I stay here?" and read to the end of the chapter. Stephanie convinces her mother that she'll be fine spending some time alone in her uncle's home. In a thrilling sequence, someone breaks into the house and attacks Stephanie. Skulduggery bursts through the door and battles the intruder, who turns out to be immune to flames. The chapter ends with Stephanie first learning about Skulduggery being a skeleton: "All he had was a skull for a head."

**Larson, Kirby.** *Hattie Big Sky.* **Delacorte, 2006. 283 p.**
Gr. 6–12. Sixteen-year-old orphan Hattie Brooks learns that she inherited a Montana homestead from an uncle whom she never met. There is a caveat: she must cultivate one-eighth of the land—forty acres—and post 480 rods of fence. She has ten months to do it, or she will lose the land. Hattie struggles with the cold, the wolves, and the attentions of a mean rancher who has his eye on Hattie's land. She also worries about the hostility her German neighbors face; the story is set in 1918. Each chapter begins with a letter or newspaper article. Pause before reading the rest of the chapter to help listeners know when the narrative begins.

   10-Minute Selection: Read the middle of chapter 4, beginning with the lines, "'There it is!' Chase called, excitement and cold shrilling his voice. 'Mr. Wright's house.'" Hattie's neighbors have given her a ride in their wagon from town to her new home. However, home turns out to be a small, worn shack. Once the neighbors leave, Hattie is discouraged. Her cat grabs a mouse and that snaps Hattie into action. "You've got your supper, Mr. Whiskers. I'd best get mine." Finish the passage with the sentence, "'Here's to our new home,' I toasted."

**Look, Lenore.** *Alvin Ho: Allergic to Girls, School, and Other Scary Things.* **Schwartz and Wade, 2008. 172 p.**
Gr. 1–4. Second-grader Alvin makes a long list of things he is afraid of. He also refuses to talk at school. These aspects about himself puzzle Alvin. He comes from a long line of Chinese "farmer-warriors who haven't had a scaredy bone in their bodies since 714 AD." His behavior causes trouble. He breaks his father's favorite toy. He imagines that his new piano teacher is actually the witch from "Hansel and Gretel." He also lets loose with a string of Shakespearean curses at his children's psychotherapist, whom he calls "the psycho."

10-Minute Selection: Read chapter 7, "The Best Way to Avoid School." Alvin learns that Jules is out of school with chicken pox. He decides to go to Jules's house to get exposed to the disease. Once in Jules's bedroom, he looks around for the chicken. Not seeing one, he settles for "the plain pox." Move on to chapter 10, "Facing the Music." We observe Alvin's father's hilarious reaction when he learns that Alvin has broken his "Johnny Astro" toy. The father cries, yells, and spews Shakespearean curses, such as "What bootless toad-spotted bladder did this?" Dad finally walks over to the piano and "played like a wild savage beast." When he stops, he decides Alvin needs piano lessons.

**Look, Lenore.** *Ruby Lu, Empress of Everything.* **Atheneum, 2006. 164 p.**
Gr. K–3. Ruby Lu's deaf cousin, Flying Duck, and her family emigrate from China and move in. "Ruby was Flying Duck's Smile Buddy at school. Smile Buddies were responsible for helping a new student feel welcome." Ruby hides letters from the school to her parents. She's afraid she has flunked second grade. Her schoolwork slips, and she joins Flying Duck in summer school to catch up on her studies. Other adventures revolve around a new dog, eye exams, learning sign language and how to swim, and her up-and-down friendship with a girl named Emma. The letters from school show up at the end of the book, informing everyone that both Ruby and Flying Duck need glasses. This is the sequel to *Ruby Lu, Brave and True.*

10-Minute Selection: Read chapter 2, "Afternoon Crafts." The first section of the chapter lists the problems Ruby has adjusting to the changes in her family's life. "'Send her back,' Ruby cried one night. . . . 'I hate immigration!'" Oscar, Ruby's little brother, sticks craft magnets up his nose and has trouble breathing. Ruby dials 911. Flying Duck succeeds in removing the magnets by sucking on Oscar's nostrils, saving the day.

**Lord, Cynthia.** *Rules.* **Scholastic, 2006. 200 p.**
Gr. 4–8. Catherine develops several rules for her younger, autistic brother, David, such as "A boy can take off his shirt to swim but not his shorts," "No toys in the fish tank," and "It's fine to hug Mom, but not the clerk at the video store." She has a big responsibility watching him while their parents work. She meets Jason, a

wheelchair-bound boy who uses word cards to communicate. She uses her artistic skills to make him more cards and expand his vocabulary. She's confused by her feelings, and her subsequent behavior causes her to risk losing her friendship with both Jason and the new girl who moves in next door.

10-Minute Selection: Read the opening chapter, which features many of the "Rules for David." We are introduced to Catherine, David, and their parents. David loves to visit the video store and becomes upset when their father is late from work. We learn about his behavior and Catherine's tactics for dealing with it. She wishes that one day David will turn into a "regular brother." The two venture next door to ask some moving men about the new neighbors. The chapter ends with David getting upset when he realizes he has to go to occupational therapy instead of the video store. "I cover David's mouth with my hand so the movers don't hear him scream."

**Lorey, Dean.** *Nightmare Academy.* **HarperCollins, 2007. 310 p.**
Gr. 4–7. Charlie learns that he possesses powers that open portals to where nightmarish creatures live. He is whisked away to a school to learn to control his power. He meets new friends, and they go on a risky journey to rescue his parents, who have been kidnapped by two of the most terrifying creatures ever. The plot and character elements seem to be taken directly from Harry Potter. There's even a large trout that sorts students by talent, much like J. K. Rowling's Sorting Hat. Regardless, this fast-paced book will keep students on the edges of their seats.

10-Minute Selection: Start reading near the end of the first chapter with the line, "It looked something like a scorpion-slick purple-black skin stretched tightly over a bloated body full to bursting with juices." Read the rest of the chapter and the entire second chapter. Charlie has uncontrollably brought a Class-5 Silvertongue into the real world. A team sent by the Nightmare Academy rescues Charlie. Charlie's father confronts the team, asking them why he shouldn't call the police. One of them replies, "Your son, Charlie, is as strong with the Gift as I've ever seen. But if he doesn't learn to control it . . . *he'll kill you all.*"

**Lowry, Lois.** *Gathering Blue.* **Houghton Mifflin, 2000. 215 p.**
Gr. 5–8. Kira's mother is dead. Her father was killed long ago. It is the custom in her community for orphans, especially those with disabilities—Kira has a deformed leg—to be sent away. A cruel woman challenges Kira's very existence in the community. Kira appears before the Council of Guardians. They assign her a new job, utilizing her weaving talents. Eventually, Kira learns that all she has been told isn't necessarily true, including events surrounding her father's death. This is a companion to Lowry's books *The Giver* and *The Messenger.*

10-Minute Selection: Inform your listeners that this story takes place possibly in the future, where things are different. Kira has just lost her mother and may be kicked out of her community because she has a deformed leg. Read the end of chapter 1, starting with the sentence, "An older child, a dirty-faced boy of eight or nine years . . ." The boy is Matt. He informs Kira that the local women want her gone. "They don't want you should stay. They be planning to turn you out, now your mum be dead." Continue reading all of chapter 2. Kira confronts Vandara, who says, "Your space is gone. It's mine now." Several women surround Kira, ready to attack. Kira evokes the law and convinces them that the conflict must go before the Council of Guardians.

**Lowry, Lois.** *Gooney Bird Greene.* **Houghton Mifflin, 2002. 88 p.**
Gr. K–4. New student Gooney Bird Greene is a storyteller extraordinaire. She also loves to be "right smack in the middle of everything." She entertains her fellow second-graders with a new story each day. "My stories are all absolutely true." Her story titles are outrageous, but Gooney Bird holds true to her claim of truthfulness through clever wordplay. Gooney's stories include "How Gooney Bird Came from China on a Flying Carpet," "The Prince, the Palace, and the Diamond Earrings," "Beloved Catman Is Consumed by a Cow," and "Why Gooney Bird Was Late for School Because She Was Directing a Symphony Orchestra." Her teacher, Mrs. Pidgeon, creates many teachable moments from Gooney Bird's stories. Gooney Bird's classmates' constant interruptions will probably appeal as much or more to adults as well as the young target audience. This is the first book in a series.

10-Minute Selection: Although any of the chapters featuring Gooney's stories will work as short selections, the first chapter will introduce Gooney, her teacher, and her quirky classmates. After reading the first chapter, continue with the second chapter, containing Gooney Bird's first story, "How Gooney Bird Got Her Name." When she was a baby, her parents compared her big feet and head-bobbing motions to a bird. They settled on the Layson Albatross but thought that was too scientific of a name to give a little girl. They chose the bird's nickname, Gooney Bird, instead.

**Lupica, Mike.** *Heat.* **Philomel, 2006. 220 p.**
Gr. 5–10. Michael Arroyo has the best fastball of any twelve-year-old in his league, but he and his older brother also carry a terrible secret. They are hiding the fact that their father recently died. The dad was driving a cab and saw a man hit a woman. After confronting the man, "he felt something grab in his chest." He drove home and died of a heart attack. His last words were, "Keep my boys together." The two brothers are all alone in New York City, and they don't want social services to separate them. Michael later becomes upset when he is accused of being older than twelve and is banned from playing. His birth certificate is back in Cuba, and there's no way to retrieve it.

10-Minute Selection: Read the first chapter. A sixteen-year-old named Ramon attacks elderly Mrs. Cora and grabs her food money. Ramon isn't the smartest or laziest boy in the South Bronx, but he is fast. And he prefers to "get his spending money stealing purses and handbags like the Hulk-green one he had in his hand right now." Ramon has no trouble outrunning the police, but he is eventually brought down by a well-thrown baseball by Michael. "'You got some arm, kid,' the cop said. 'That's what they tell me,' Michael said."

**Mackel, Kathy.** *MadCat.* **HarperCollins, 2005. 185 p.**
Gr. 4–8. MadCat is a twelve-year-old who lives for her softball team, the Sting. The new season, however, brings several changes. Some aggressive parents have reorganized the team to make a serious effort to make the National Fastpitch Softball World Series. These changes mean that some of the regular players have been replaced by former rivals. At least one ringer has been added to the roster. Even their old coach has been replaced. MadCat keeps working hard for the team, but she also worries about her friend Mugger, who didn't make the team; another friend, Jess, who is hiding something; and her father, who has been diagnosed with multiple sclerosis.

10-Minute Selection: Read chapter 13, which opens with the sentence, "We were just so good." MadCat is trying hard to keep her new teammates straight and to also hang on to her position as the starting catcher. She and Ivy compete in throwing out base stealers. She senses a change when Mr. Reed challenges Coach Mac to keep up the contest. "Mac glared at him. 'The girls need to sit down. They're hot.' 'They're hot to compete,' Mr. Reed said, glaring back. 'We'd be fools to stop that.'" The competition turns up a notch. There's a sense that Coach Mac's days are numbered as he walks off the field as Mr. Reed says, "That, my dear ladies, is how you play to win."

**Maguire, Gregory.** *Leaping Beauty and Other Animal Fairy Tales.*
**HarperCollins, 2004. 197 p.**
Gr. K–6. Author Maguire recasts eight popular folk tales with hilarious animal characters. Titles include "So What and the Seven Giraffes," "Rumplesnakeskin," "Hamster and Gerbil," "Cinder-Elephant," "The Three Little Penguins and the Big Bad Walrus," and "Little Red Robin Hood," who brings his granny a basket of "worm brandy, the worm casserole, and the wormy cheese." The title story features Old Dame Hornet cursing a newborn frog princess. Some beetles alter the curse, and the princess becomes known as "Weeping Beauty." The wise king and queen set their noisy, crying infant under the home of the hornet, the curse gets altered a few more times, and the baby becomes a dancer known as "Leaping Beauty."

10-Minute Selection: All the stories are great to share with a wide range of audiences. "Goldiefox and the Three Chickens" made me laugh out loud a few more times than the other tales. The chickens live in a house in the forest. When they go out for a walk, an out-of-work carpenter fox eats their oatmeal, destroys their chairs (getting one stuck on his foot), and breaks their beds (getting one stuck on his other foot). When Mama Hen sees Papa Rooster's chair, she states, "'I sometimes feel like jumping up and down on things and breaking them. But I choose to control my temper when I feel like that. It's my best quality, patience.' Then she saw her own chair and lost her patience." In the end, they make a deal with the fox and open the Three Chickens Furniture Store and Oatmeal Restaurant.

**Maguire, Gregory. *Three Rotten Eggs.* Clarion, 2002. 184 p.**
Gr. 4–6. A rough boy named Thaddeus "Thud" Nero Tweed—"TNT" for short— arrives at Miss Earth's classroom. The balance between the two class clubs, the Copycats (the boys) and the Tattletales (the girls), is threatened by several events. During a school charity egg hunt, the kids find three eggs. The eggs are warm. The kids care for them, and when the eggs hatch, everyone is in for a big surprise. "Then it opened its little beak and emitted a small jet of fire, about as strong as a cigarette lighter's flame." The eggs have been genetically altered. This is the fifth book in Maguire's Hamlet Chronicles.

    10-Minute Selection: Read a section of chapter 3, "Thud Tweed." The class meets Thud for the first time. Start with the line, "I'm looking for Earth's class," and proceed to the end of the chapter. Thud warns his teacher, "Why don't I move my desk out here in the hall and sit down? I'll get in trouble and you'll just be moving me out here by lunchtime anyway. Let's save time. In fact, I'd like to apply to be expelled right away." The newcomer manages to insensitively insult each class member in the few minutes Miss Earth is gone from the room.

**Marcantonio, Patricia Santos. *Red Ridin' in the Hood and Other Cuentos.* Farrar Straus Giroux, 2005. 181 p.**
Gr. 3–12. Several traditional European and Middle Eastern folktales are retold with a Latino cultural spin. A few are set in contemporary times, such as "Juan and the Pinto Bean Stalk" ("Jack and the Beanstalk"), "Emperador's New Clothes" ("The Emperor's New Clothes"), and the title story, which finds Roja taking goodies to her *abuelita* and running into Lobo Chavez on Forest Street. Other retellings include "The Three Chicharrones" ("The Three Pigs"), "Blanca Nieves and the Seven Vaqueritos" ("Snow White and the Seven Dwarfs"), and six more. Of particular interest is "The Sleeping Beauty" story told from the viewpoint of the *bruja*, or witch, who cast the spell. "I really didn't want to be bad in the first place. It's just that no one ever gave me a chance to be nice or good." A glossary is provided for the many Spanish terms woven into the stories.

    10-Minute Selection: Every story in this collection works as a 10-Minute Selection. Start with the opening story, "Jaime and Gabriela," a retelling of "Hansel and Gretel." The children's father is a poor adobe maker who is facing hard times. His second wife convinces him to take the children into the desert and leave them. The children find a house made of *pan dulce* and tamales. Both the evil stepmother and the witch, Señora Sombra, turn into fireballs when defeated.

**Marsden, Carolyn.** *Moon Runner.* **Candlewick, 2005. 97 p.**
Gr. 3–5. Mina is new to school, but she's quickly welcomed into the Fellow Friends, a small group of friends. She never considered herself athletic. One day during gym, Mina is surprised to learn that she loves running. And she does it very well. The only problem is that one of the Fellow Friends, Ruth, considers herself to be *the* athlete of the group. Mina worries that her newfound athleticism might cost her some friends.

10-Minute Selection: Read the very short chapter 6, which describes how Mina got her nickname, Moon Runner. Mina created a picture of the moon. Mina's father asks her to demonstrate her running abilities when he hears that she tied for first place in a running contest. Mina's sister Paige runs over with the moon picture. "Mina . . . stood up and put her hands on her hips. She smiled to herself. *Moon Runner.* She liked the sound." Follow this with a reading of chapter 8. Mina goes jogging with her mother and reveals her concerns about competing against Ruth. "If I win, our Fellow Friends group will fall apart for sure. . . . If I let Ruth win, I'll feel icky about myself."

**McCaughrean, Geraldine.** *Cyrano.* **Harcourt, 2006. 114 p.**
Gr. 8–12. Author McCaughrean re-creates the story of Cyrano de Bergerac, a captain of the French army and a poet. Cyrano is known for his large nose and, because of it, never approaches his cousin Roxane to tell her of his love. Roxane falls in love with Christian, one of Cyrano's new cadets. Cyrano helps Christian articulate their love of Roxane. Also in love with Roxane is the wealthy and powerful Comte de Guiche, who sets plans in motion for Cyrano and Christian to face certain death in battle.

10-Minute Selection: Read the first half of chapter 1, "A Night at the Theatre." This chapter contains the famous list of ten insults that Cyrano makes if he were to make fun of his own nose. "Or Nine! The Insult Unsporting: You must be the only man who can win a race by a nose before the starter has even fired his gun!" End with the line, "Then, in the swish of a silken gown, she was gone, and it was as if one of the great multi-tiered chandeliers had blown out in the draught." Move on to the chapter titled "Christian." Begin with the sentence, "So give us the account of 'One Hundred Against One'!" Cyrano reads his poem, where he faced several attackers alone. Christian ends Cyrano's sentences for him with hilarious references to Cyrano's nose. Finish with the line, "It's just that the others dared me to."

**McCaughrean, Geraldine.** *The Kite Rider.* **HarperCollins, 2001. 272 p.**
Gr. 5–10. Haoyou witnesses the death of his father and then becomes a kite rider for a traveling circus in thirteenth-century China. As a kite rider, Haoyou is strapped to a large kite and flown high into the air—a very dangerous stunt, but one that Haoyou becomes very accomplished at. His hair-raising adventures include escaping the clutches of the man he believes murdered his father, being terrorized in the air by a weapon-carrying kite rider, and almost losing his head to Kubla Khan himself.

10-Minute Selection: Read most of chapter 10, "The Paddy." Start with the sentences, "What is it? What's the matter?" and read until the end of the chapter. A toddler has wandered away from the circus near some paddy fields. Haoyou volunteers to fly above in his kite to spot the missing child. In doing so, he crashes and finds the kite pinning him underwater. "The blow knocked all the air out of him. He could not have drawn breath even if he had not been facedown in thickly dirty water. He fumbled with the belt buckle that secured him to the kite, but there was no freeing it."

**McDonald, Megan.** *Judy Moody.* **Candlewick, 2000. 160 p.**
Gr. K–3. Judy is initially angry that summer is ending. She's also not crazy about starting third grade. "Judy Moody was in a mood. Not a good mood. A bad mood. A mad-face mood." She eventually gets into the swing of things thanks to her teacher, Mr. Todd, whom Judy calls Mr. Toad. She works hard on her "Me" collage. She also tries to think of a way to avoid attending "Frank Eats-Paste Pearl's birthday party." Judy, her friend Rocky, and her little brother, Stink, start an exclusive club called the Toad Pee Club. To be a member, one holds a toad in his or her hands until it pees. This is the first book in the successful Judy Moody series.

10-Minute Selection: Read the chapter titled "My Favorite Pet." Judy goes to the pet store with her family. " 'Do you have any two-toed sloths?' she asked the pet-store lady. 'Sorry. Fresh out,' said the lady." Judy instead buys a Venus flytrap. Stink wants to name it Bughead. Continue reading the next chapter, "My Smelly Pet." Judy takes her Venus flytrap to school. It stinks up her backpack. She decides on a name—Jaws!

**McDonald, Megan.** *Stink and the Incredible Super-Galactic Jawbreaker.*
**Candlewick, 2006. 118 p.**
Gr. K–4. Stink uses the letter-writing skills he learned in school for personal gain. He complains to a candy company that a jawbreaker didn't break his jaw. In return, he receives "a big box full of . . . jawbreakers!" He writes to other businesses and receives more packages until his mother says, "no more letters." Stink also gets a present from his grandmother—glow-in-the-dark pajamas for Pajama Day at school. Unfortunately, "one wash and all the glow stuff rubbed off." At school,

he is mystified at the cold shoulder he receives from his best friend. This is one in a series of books about Judy Moody's little brother, Stink.

10-Minute Selection: Read the chapter titled "Finger Lickin' Good." Stink licks and licks and licks his giant jawbreaker. "Stink's jawbreaker went from super-galactic to just plain galactic. From golf-ball size to Super-Ball size." He eats it until it's the size of a "teeny-tiny pea." He then writes his letter complaining, "It did NOT (I repeat NOT) break my jaw." Follow this by reading the entire next chapter, "A Leopard Can't Change Its Spots." Stink receives his box containing 21,280 jawbreakers with an apology from the company. McDonald's lines are a joy to read aloud. "Holy jawbreaker heaven . . . mega jawbreakers, mini jawbreakers, monster jawbreakers, black, rainbow, and psychedelic jawbreakers . . ."

**Mercado, Nancy E., ed.** *Tripping Over the Lunch Lady and Other School Stories.* **Dial, 2004. 177 p.**
Gr. 4–10. This collection contains ten stories that highlight the humorous and sometimes heartbreaking aspects of school life. Rachel Vail's story, "The Crush," features a boy who accidentally injures a girl named Gabriela during a sports event. He tells her how much he enjoyed her "dust mite feces report." David Lubar's story, "Science Friction," introduces four oddly matched students working together on a science project. They meet in the narrator's bedroom after school. "Wow. It's sort of like you live inside a laundry basket." From the mess they make in his room, they develop a project about mold. The title story, by Angela Johnson, follows the class klutz, known as Jinx. "I've broken my arm making cookies. Don't ask. I even got locked in my own locker once." Be sure to share each author's "school report" at the end of each chapter, where they share their favorite and least favorite class, best prank played, and more.

10-Minute Selection: Although most of the stories make fun stand-alone reads—the exceptions being Avi's story, which is full of hard-to-read intentional misspellings, and James Proimos's comic-format story—Terry Trueman's "Apple Blossoms" will get the most laughs. The class clown tries hard to read his poem with a straight face but manages to crack up his fellow students when he repeatedly (and unintentionally) mispronounces "apple blossoms" as "assel bloppems."

**Michael, Livi.** *City of Dogs.* **Putnam, 2007. 256 p.**
Gr. 5–8. The great battle to end the world may be coming to Earth because of the actions of the dog Jenny. She saved Baldur, a Norse god, and her master from death, which set a terrible chain of events into motion. She travels to Earth and meets a new master, Sam. She also forms a pack of unique, charismatic dogs that helps save the world from destruction. They encounter characters from Norse and Greek mythology during their quest, including Cerberus, the three-headed dog, and the wolves that plan to swallow the sun and moon.

10-Minute Selection: Any of the early chapters that introduce the various dogs are fun chapters to share, particularly the chapter about Gentleman Jim, who wakes up his master: "[He] would unroll his massive tongue, containing over half a pint of drool, and dribble it slowly into his ear." A chapter that gives a better sense of the whole book is chapter 17, "Black Shuck." It follows the quest of dogs Checkers and Boris. They meet Black Shuck, a large supernatural dog, who is amused that these two small dogs want to battle a larger dog known as the Guardian of the Darkest Way (Cerberus). Boris is fairly flippant with his reactions to Black Shuck, who decides to show them the way to the underworld. The long chapter ends with the line, "And at that moment the caves began to moan."

**Miller, Sarah.** *Miss Spitfire: Reaching Helen Keller.* **Atheneum, 2007. 208 p.**
Gr. 5–10. Annie Sullivan was only twenty years old when she accepted the job of teaching young Helen Keller in this fictional account of the famous true story. We learn of Annie's childhood hardships as well as her attempts to communicate with the deaf, blind, and spoiled six-year-old. Annie tries to teach Helen as well as Helen's family, who always give in to Helen's tantrums. Even though she feels like giving up several times, Annie's tenacity earns her the nickname Miss Spitfire.

10-Minute Selection: Read chapter 7, which opens with this quote from one of Anne Sullivan's letters: "She is never still a moment." Annie is appalled at Helen's manners at the dinner table. Annie has self-doubts and thinks, "I'm not sure I can do this job." The next morning, the two are working on a lesson upstairs. Helen successfully locks Annie in the bedroom and hides the key. Continue reading the first two pages of the next chapter. Annie is rescued—"carried out the window and down the ladder like a sack of potatoes"—and humiliated. End with the line, "Just as soon as the captain hangs my bedroom door."

**Morgenstern, Susie.** *A Book of Coupons.* **Viking, 2001. 62 p.**
Gr. 3–5. Monsieur Noel, the new teacher at the Marie Curie School in France, surprises his students on the first day of the school year. His first words to them are, "I have a present for you." The present turns out to be a book of coupons for each student—coupons for astonishing things, such as "One coupon for being late to school," "One coupon for making a lot of noise," and "One coupon for taking your own sweet time." The coupons and Monsieur Noel's teaching methods do not sit well with the strict principal, Incarnation Perez.

10-Minute Selection: Read the first several pages of this unchaptered novella. The kids overcome their initial disappointment in their teacher when they receive the coupons. They are a little unsure when they receive a second gift—a copy of *David Copperfield*. "Everyone started hunting frantically for a 'coupon for not reading a book' in vain." One student, Charles, winds up staying "up past midnight reading *David Copperfield*." In the morning, he hands his mother his coupon for sleeping in late. "What could she do but give in?" End the passage with the sentence, "Okay, you can have it in exchange for three other coupons."

**Morpurgo, Michael.** *Private Peaceful.* **Scholastic, 2003. 202 p.**
Gr. 7–12. Two brothers, Charlie and Tommo Peaceful, sign up to fight for England in World War I. Tommo recounts tales of the boys' lives, their mother, their father (who was killed in an accident), their mentally handicapped brother, the girl they both fell in love with, and their cruel great-aunt and just-as-cruel landowner. There are vivid war scenes. Through it all, Tommo remembers Charlie's strong convictions and how this trait ultimately led to his downfall. Be sure to read the endnotes, where the author tells of the English soldiers who were executed for desertion, cowardice, and even sleeping at their posts.

10-Minute Selection: Read the middle section of the chapter titled "Twenty-Eight Minutes Past One," beginning with the sentence, "As I came around the corner I saw them," and reading through the lines, "I had to prove myself. I had to prove myself to myself." Tommo is in town when marching soldiers arrive. A sergeant major tries to recruit local young men to join because they are needed to fight the Germans. "Because, mark my words, ladies and gentlemen, if we don't stop them out in France the Germans will be here, right here in Hatherleigh, right here on your doorstep." A few men step forward. An old woman behind fifteen-year-old Tommo prods him and says, "Go on. Y'ain't a coward, are you?" Tommo runs away but later decides to enlist when he learns Charlie is going, too.

**Morris, Gerald.** *The Adventures of Sir Lancelot the Great.* **Houghton Mifflin, 2008. 92 p.**
Gr. 2–6. Sir Lancelot leaves his home in France to join King Arthur in Camelot. He's upset when he gets muddy on his travels, and he begins cleaning himself. While he does so, he unhorses knight after knight who come charging him— sixteen in total. It turns out he found himself in a tournament sponsored by King Arthur. Lancelot has other adventures, including being captured by four queens, defending Queen Guinevere's life, getting shot by an arrow in his behind, and entering a tournament incognito as the Knight of the Pillow. This is the first book in Morris's Knight's Tales series.

10-Minute Selection: Read the funny second chapter, "The Fastest Knight in England." Lancelot is tricked into taking off his armor and leaving his weapons behind as he climbs a tree to rescue a damsel's falcon. Once in the tree, Lancelot learns that he is trapped. Sir Phelot plans to slay Lancelot the moment he climbs down. Lancelot refuses to come down and starts tossing acorns off of Phelot's armor. Sir Phelot decides to cut the tree down, gets his sword stuck, turns around, and faces an armed Lancelot. Sir Phelot becomes famous for how fast he runs from Lancelot. Reading the damsel's lines where she sobs is especially fun: "WIBBLE-BLIDDER-WO-WO-HAH-WAAH!"

**Morris, Gerald. *The Lioness and Her Knight*. Houghton Mifflin, 2005. 340 p.**
Gr. 4–10. This Arthurian story has it all—romance, adventure, and humor. Sixteen-year-old Lady Luneta leaves her family estate, escorted by her cousin Ywain. A fool named Rhience joins them, and all three find plenty of adventure. Luneta is nearly burned as a witch, all three are nearly killed by two brutish brothers, Ywain befriends a lioness, and Luneta becomes an enchantress under the tutelage of Morgan LeFay. This is one book in Morris's Squire's Tales series.

10-Minute Selection: Read the hilarious opening of the book. Luneta is spying on her parents. She clearly gets her wit from her father. Luneta has secretly insulted her mother with a Latin phrase. "[Y]ou will oblige me very much if you refrain from calling your mother 'little piggy' even in Latin." Stop at the line, "Then he said, 'Certainly not,' and left." Move on to the last section of chapter 9, "Questing." Begin with the sentence, "The path took them through quiet forests and over barren heaths," and finish the chapter. Luneta and Rhience have traveled to a land where every peasant hurls insults at them. "You best keep her away from the kiddies at night or they'll never sleep, thinking of her uglies." The two learn why they are subjected to such language by the end of the chapter.

**Murdock, Catherine Gilbert. *Dairy Queen*. Houghton Mifflin, 2006. 275 p.**
Gr. 6–10. Fifteen-year-old D.J. Schwenk is having a lousy summer. She lives on a dairy farm near Red Bend, Wisconsin. Her father's injury and her brothers' absences mean that she's responsible for most of the farm chores. She's also been asked by a family friend to help train Brian, the quarterback of the rival football team. She's played sports with her brothers her whole life. After Brian compares her to a cow, D.J. realizes that she'll only find happiness if she tries out for the Red Bend boy's football team. The sequel is titled *The Off Season*.

10-Minute Selection: Read a few selections that show how D.J. cleared part of the farm to make a football field. Start a little into chapter 12 with the line, "The next morning, as everyone except me was getting ready for church . . ." and read until the sentence, "If that thought had been a fly, I would have killed it with a fly swatter." Pick up the selection in chapter 13 when Brian sees the field for the first time. Start with the sentence, "Boy, you should have seen Brian's face," and read until the end of the chapter.

**Myers, Walter Dean. *Harlem Summer*. Scholastic, 2007. 151 p.**
Gr. 6–12. It's hot in Harlem the summer of 1925. Aspiring jazz musician Mark Purvis has encounters with several famous people of the time through an almost

comic series of blunders. He's hired by jazz great Fats Waller to unload a truck. Unfortunately, the truck goes missing, and Mark's life is in danger from mobster Dutch Schultz. While trying to survive, Mark rubs shoulders with the likes of W. E. B. DuBois and Langston Hughes. Mark's father sums up the summer when he says, "Mark, you are a young black man. Sometimes, living here in Harlem, we walk on the sunny side of the street and sometimes we walk on the shady side." This is a great supplemental read for a group studying the Harlem Renaissance.

10-Minute Selection: Read the chapter titled "Things Are Looking Up Until We Find a Dead Watermelon at the End of the Rainbow." Mark and his friends audition for Black Swan Records. On their way out, they meet two white guys who want them to check out their club. The three boys take a ride and find out that the men work for Dutch Schultz. The gangster fires three shots at a watermelon as a warning that the boys should pay him his money. "That's when I started to pee. Not a lot. Just a little." Then Schultz says, "Now why don't you boys go on out of here and get what you owe me?" Mark hesitates before rising. "I got up. I was crying a little and peeing a little. Just a little."

**Myers, Walter Dean.** *Sunrise over Fallujah.* **Scholastic, 2008. 282 p.**
Gr. 6–12. Robin, aka Birdy, a young man from Harlem, enlists in the army and is assigned to Civilian Affairs. It's 2003 and America is about to invade Iraq. The unit's job is to act "as a liaison between the military and the civilians in a war zone or disaster area." They are never completely sure what's going on with the big picture. "Over and over I thought we were in a war of complete randomness." Their unit is then handpicked to take part in a risky exchange involving kidnapped tribal children.

10-Minute Selection: The chapters are not titled or numbered. Go to page 71 of the hardcover edition. Begin with the lines, "The portable toilet facilities stunk and the small cabin was filled with tiny flies that bit my butt. But it was the sounds of incoming mortars that shook me the most." The unit is commanded to transport some prisoners, including an old man who was taken because he had an AK-47 in his house. Their Humvee gets stuck in foul-smelling mud, but several Iraqi men pull them out with rope and a mule. "'Birdy, this is embarrassing!' Marla said as the guy tied the rope around the mules' halter." Finish with the sentence, "It had been that kind of day."

Second 10-Minute Selection: Begin on page 159 with the line, "The first Humvee driver knew his way pretty well, and we reached the Old City area in quick time." The unit believes they have raided an innocent family until Marla finds several detonators hidden in a container of flour. End with the sentence, "I remembered how bad I felt for them, only to find out that they were in a family that probably would have killed me if they had the chance."

**Nagdo, Ann Whitehead.** *Tarantula Power.* **Holiday House, 2007. 93 p.**
Gr. 1–4. Richard is upset that his classmate Kevin is picking on a second-grader named Sam. He is also perturbed to learn that their teacher made Kevin his "Invent a Cereal" project partner. "Richard groaned. The thought of working with Kevin made him want to barf." Richard tries different tactics to make Kevin stop picking on Sam, but he eventually gets inspiration from the classroom pet, a tarantula named Ruby, in helping Sam confront his tormentor. "I have tarantula fangs for you to wear when you feel scared,' said Richard. 'They will make you feel brave.'"

10-Minute Selection: Read chapter 2. Mrs. Steele introduces the class to their new pet tarantula. "'I have a surprise for you.' Mrs. Steele picked up a shopping bag. 'A friend of mine has given us a class pet.'" Move on to a few pages in chapter 6, starting with the line, "When Richard got to the library, he went over to Nando, the librarian," and read to the end of the chapter. Richard discovers a recipe for "cricket brownies" and plans on getting back at Kevin, who has been stealing Sam's brownies. The selection ends with the sentence, "And when he eats it, he'll get a big, crunchy surprise."

**Naidoo, Beverley.** *The Other Side of Truth.* **HarperCollins, 2000. 248 p.**
Gr. 5–11. Twelve-year-old Sade and her younger brother, Fermi, are smuggled out of their homeland of Nigeria after their mother is murdered. Their journalist father has been a sharp critic of the military government. Once the children arrive in London, the woman who accompanied them abandons them. They were going to stay with their uncle, but he has disappeared. They are finally picked up and placed in foster care. Sade faces her own bullies at school. When their father makes it to England, he is placed in prison, with the threat of being deported back to Nigeria hanging over his head. The sequel is titled *Web of Lies.*

10-Minute Selection: Before reading, inform your audience that young Sade and her brother flew from Nigeria to London with a smuggler and that they were quickly abandoned. Now the children are all alone in the strange city. They can't go to the authorities for fear of being deported back to a murderous government. Read chapter 10, "Thieves and Vandals." The children are walking the city streets, trying to figure out what to do. "If anyone asked where they came from and what they were doing, whatever should they say?" They are robbed by a man in an alley and then accused by the owner of a video store of helping some vandals. "Well, you can tell your story to the police!"

**Napoli, Donna Jo, and Robert Furrow.** *Sly the Sleuth and the Sports Mysteries.*
**Dial, 2006. 126 p.**
Gr. K–4. A young girl named Sly runs the detective agency Sleuth for Hire and tries to solve three neighborhood mysteries. The first case involves a mystery of

why birds flock around the soccer field when Jack wants to practice. Sly accidentally hits a bird with the soccer ball, and the ball bounces into the net. The second
case revolves around missing ballet slippers and swim fins and a pair of baseball
cleats. This is one in a series of Sly the Sleuth books.

10-Minute Selection: Read the third mystery, "Sly and the Basketball Blues."
Sly and other girls start a cheerleading squad for the school's basketball teams.
They won't let Brian join the squad. When Brian starts acting strangely, his
mother asks Sly to figure out why. Brian had a friend "roll him" with a rolling pin.
Next, Brian hung from branches with a roll of duct tape with magnets around his
ankles. Finally, Brian tried to spend all day in the bathtub to swell up like rice. It
turns out that Brian is trying to become taller to play basketball. In the end, Brian
becomes the squad's mascot.

**Naylor, Phyllis Reynolds.** *Polo's Mother.* **Atheneum, 2005. 162 p.**
Gr. 2–5. A cat named Polo finally meets his mother, Geraldine, who turns out
to be a wisecracking roamer. "I seem to be in a garage of some sort with a pip-
squeak here who claims to be my son." Texas Jake, leader of the "Club of Mysteries," challenges Geraldine. He has her answer mysteries in order to be allowed to
stay, such as "What is dust?" Geraldine replies, "Why, everyone knows that dust is
made up of cat hair, dog hair, and little star babies falling out of the sky." Geraldine and Texas Jake constantly argue. This causes the leader to turn his anger on
Polo and send the little cat to solve a dangerous mystery. This is the fourth book
in the Cat Pack series.

10-Minute Selection: Start in the middle of chapter 4, "A Bold Plan," with the
sentence, "When they woke the next morning, Geraldine was gone." Geraldine
actually has gone off to find a refrigerator to solve the third challenge from Texas
Jake: does the light stay on when the refrigerator door is closed? Continue reading
chapter 5, "One Cold Cat." Geraldine is trapped inside a working refrigerator, and
Polo asks Crow to help save her. Finish where the frozen Geraldine haltingly says
the line, "When . . . the refrigerator door . . . is closed . . . the light . . . goes . . . off."

**Naylor, Phyllis Reynolds.** *Roxie and the Hooligans.* **Atheneum, 2006. 116 p.**
Gr. 1–4. Roxie Warbler looks forward to visits from Uncle Dangerfoot. Her uncle
is an adventurer who travels with Lord Thistlebottom, the author of Roxie's favorite book, *Lord Thistlebottom's Book of Pitfalls and How to Survive Them.* Unfortunately, Roxie is the target of a gang of bullies, headed by Helvetia Hagus.
Roxie and the hoodlums fall into a dumpster, which gets loaded onto a ship. They
are dumped into the sea and swim to an island. There are two robbers on the island. The kids overhear one of the robbers state, "Anybody on this island besides
us, I'll slit his throat." Roxie helps the other kids survive by remembering survival
tips from Lord Thistlebottom's book.

10-Minute Selection: Read the second half of the first chapter, "Uncle Dangerfoot," starting with the sentence, "She took a little of the water and pulled the covers up under her chin." We meet the hooligans who torment Roxie. After finishing the chapter, tell your students that Roxie finds herself stranded on a deserted island with the bullies. Read the chapter titled "A Slimy Sandwich." Roxie shows the hooligans how to survive by eating a grub.

**O'Connor, Barbara. *How to Steal a Dog*. Farrar Straus Giroux, 2007. 170 p.**
Gr. 3–6. Georgina, her mother, and her little brother are homeless and live in a car. The kids have to do their homework with a flashlight, and everyone cleans up the best they can in gas-station bathrooms. Georgina gets the idea to steal a dog in hopes that the owner will pay Georgina a handsome reward. She starts writing down instructions for stealing a dog in her notebook. She finally spots the perfect dog to steal.

10-Minute Selection: Explain to your listeners that Georgina is homeless, and in desperation she steals a dog for the reward money. Read chapter 10, where Georgina actually steals Willy from his owner, Carmella Whitmore. Georgina and her brother, Toby, hide the dog in an abandoned house. Toby starts to argue, but Georgina convinces him that her plan is the only way they'll be able to raise enough money to live in a real house. The chapter ends with Georgina having second thoughts about her actions. "But it was getting hard to get my thoughts all straightened out with my insides kicking up like they were. That tapping feeling was turning into full-out banging."

**Park, Linda Sue. *Archer's Quest*. Clarion, 2006. 159 p.**
Gr. 4–6. Kevin is shocked when a strangely garbed man shows up in his bedroom. He eventually learns the stranger is the ancient Korean leader Chu-mong, whom Kevin dubs Archer. Archer tries to comprehend the modern world. He believes glass is invisible pottery and that cars are carts that contain dragons. Kevin desperately tries to help Archer return back to his own time. "'Archer, please,' he said. 'You know you're not in your own country anymore, right? Everything's different—the glass, the bed—it's a different place. I know this place better than you do, and you're gonna have to trust me when I tell you that you *can't* walk home.'"

10-Minute Selection: Read chapter 1. Kevin is studying when an arrow appears out of nowhere and pins his baseball cap against the wall. Archer has fired a warning shot. All Kevin knows is that a stranger is in his house, and he must somehow call 911. Continue reading the first section of chapter 2. Archer has fired another arrow, which breaks a window. Kevin succeeds in calming Archer down and learns a little more about the man. End the selection at the line, "'My father tried to kill me,' he said."

**Park, Linda Sue.** *Project Mulberry.* **Clarion, 2005. 221 p.**
Gr. 3–5. Julia and her best friend, Patrick, need a project for their Wiggle Club, a 4-H-type program designed to teach kids about farming. Patrick is excited to raise silkworms. Julia is worried that the project is "too Korean." "I didn't want to do something weird and Asian for the Wiggle Club. I wanted a nice, normal, All-American, red-white-and-blue kind of project." She finally agrees to work on the silkworm project. She is excited about embroidering something out of the silk the worms produce. After the silkworm eggs hatch and the kids watch the worms make their cocoons, Julia is stunned to learn that the only way to harvest the silk is to kill the cocoons. Your audience will also enjoy the insight Linda Sue Park gives with the in-between-chapter dialogue between Park and her fictional protagonist, Julia.

10-Minute Selection: Read the last half of chapter 4, starting with the sentence, "Patrick and I have done lots of projects together." Julia expresses her concerns about the project. We also experience her relationship with her younger brother, Kenny. Listeners will laugh at Julia's nickname for Kenny: Snotbrain. That passage is a setup to chapter 9, when Patrick wisely enlists Kenny to help with the silkworm project, against Julia's protests. The chapter ends with Julia worrying, "But still, all we had were eggs. When were we going to have worms?"

**Paterson, Katherine.** *The Same Stuff as Stars.* **Clarion, 2002. 242 p.**
Gr. 4–6. Eleven-year-old Angel is responsible for her younger brother, Bernie, because their father is in jail and their mother, Verna, is very self-centered. After visiting their father in prison, Verna makes the kids pack their suitcases. She dumps them at their great-grandmother's rural home and leaves without saying good-bye. This is the first time the children have met Grandma, and Angel finds herself mothering her along with her brother. Angel also meets a mysterious man in a nearby field at night watching the stars with his telescope. He teaches her that people are made out of the same stuff as stars.

10-Minute Selection: Read chapter 13. Angel makes arrangements for the two kids to enroll in school. Grandma winds up walking Bernie to the bus stop because the kindergarten bus comes later in the day. Angel rebuffs another student who approaches her. "*I don't want friends,* she told herself. *Friends get nosy. I don't want to have to explain about Verna.*" After school, Angel panics when Grandma is not at home. It turns out that Grandma spent the whole day in kindergarten and is irritable. She climbs down from the school bus with Bernie, who says, "I was the only kid at school with a grandma in my class all day!"

**Paulsen, Gary.** *Brian's Hunt.* **Wendy Lamb, 2003. 99 p.**
Gr. 4–8. Brian, from the extremely popular series that began with Paulsen's book *Hatchet,* is heading back to the Canadian wilderness. He is alone with his canoe and supplies, including his bow and arrow. He finds a wounded domesticated dog

in the middle of the woods and administers first aid. The two become companions. Brian heads for a Cree summer camp, but upon arriving, he finds his friends dead at their cabin, attacked by a bear. Brian rescues the daughter and vows to find and kill the bear. One doesn't need to have read the previous title about Brian to enjoy this book.

10-Minute Selection: Read chapter 4. It opens with the line, "A strange sound awakened him." Brian had been sleeping in his canoe when he hears the dog whimpering in the middle of the night. As Brian paddles toward the dog, he sees that she has been wounded. "It had bled all down her side, and much of the blood had clotted, but in the moonlight Brian could see the shine of fresh blood." Inform your listeners that Brian sews the wound closed and the dog tolerates it. Move on to chapter 6. Brian looks around for signs that would explain the mystery of the dog's presence. He also hunts a rabbit and catches some pan fish to help the dog recover. Brian decides to head north to the Cree camp. The passage ends with Brian looking forward to a leisurely trip: "But still he found himself pushing, hurrying, and he didn't really know why."

**Paulsen, Gary.** *How Angel Peterson Got His Name and Other Outrageous Tales about Extreme Sports.* **Wendy Lamb, 2003. 111 p.**
Gr. 4–9. Paulsen claims that he and his boyhood contemporaries were doing extreme sports back in the 1940s and 1950s, long before their current popularity. However, he states that "1. We were quite a bit dumber then. 2. There wasn't any safety gear." These humorous short stories based on Paulsen's memories will entertain both boys and girls. The title story features Carl "Angel" Peterson. Carl got his nickname after "skiing" with a rope and skis tied to the back of a '39 Ford sedan at upwards of eighty miles an hour. After a spectacular wipeout, Carl stated he heard angels sing. Other stories show how the boys did the equivalent of bungee jumping, hang gliding, and barrel jumping.

10-Minute Selection: Read chapter 4, "Girls and the Circle of Death." The county fair features a bear-wrestling act. People could win twenty-five dollars if they stay in the ring for one minute with Bruno, a muzzled bear. Young Orvis takes up the challenge to impress a group of girls. He wins on his second attempt but only after he's tossed all over by Bruno. The chapter ends with a wobbly Orvis asking, "Wasn't I wearing shoes when we came?"

**Pearsall, Shelley.** *All Shook Up.* **Knopf, 2008. 255 p.**
Gr. 5–8. Thirteen-year-old Josh is shocked to learn that his father has turned into an Elvis Presley impersonator. Josh has been living in Boston with his mother ever since his parents' divorce. Circumstances send him to Chicago to stay with his father for some time. He worries about school; trying hard to fit in with the right crowd is important to Josh. Instead, he meets Ivory, his father's girlfriend's

daughter. She is an independent girl who hangs with the artistic crowd. Josh is horrified when he learns his father has been asked to perform as Elvis at his school. He sets up a devious plan to avoid being embarrassed as the kid whose father pretended to be Elvis.

10-Minute Selection: Read the short chapter 20, "Watch Out for an Expected Surprise." Josh thinks that things are going well. He hit a home run in gym and got invited to sit with the cool kids in the lunchroom. Then he learns that the music director hired his dad to perform at school. Continue with chapter 21, "Words." Josh is determined to come up with a plan so that his father doesn't show up at school. "There's a line in an Elvis song about being caught in a trap with no way out. Just like in the song, I was caught. And there was no good way out. Somebody was going to get hurt by whatever I did."

**Peck, Richard.** *On the Wings of Heroes.* **Dial, 2007. 148 p.**
Gr. 4–8. Everyone in Davey Bowman's Illinois town makes sacrifices during World War II. Davey's older brother, Bill, goes off to war. Davey and his friend collect scrap materials for the war effort. A feisty old woman becomes Davey's new teacher after a gang of female bullies runs off the regular teacher. Chicago gangsters make a brief appearance in town. And Davey's somewhat pushy grandparents move in with his family shortly before they all receive a telegram stating that Bill is missing in action.

10-Minute Selection: Read the very short chapter titled "The Street." Davey's father thwarts a bunch of boys who plan on smashing the family's pumpkin on Halloween. Read the next chapter, "The Last Halloween." It features another time Davey's father outwits a Halloween prankster. A fun alternate chapter is "Scooter Put a Pin in Midway Island." Davey and Scooter climb into Mr. Stonecypher's attic to fetch an old brass bed. Mr. Stonecypher himself is quite a character. "Don't stand in the door. Come on in. You're letting the flies out."

**Peck, Richard.** *Past Perfect, Present Tense: New and Collected Stories.* **Dial, 2004. 177 p.**
Gr. 5–12. Don't let the bland cover stop you from sharing this rich collection of short stories. Many of Richard Peck's best short stories can be found here, including his modern-day young adult classics "Priscilla and the Wimps" and "Shotgun Cheatham's Last Night above Ground," which later evolved into Peck's award-winning novel *A Long Way from Chicago.* After the first story, the collection is divided into three sections: "The Past," "The Supernatural," and "The Present." Be sure to also read Peck's reflections about how the stories came to be written as well as his five invaluable writing hints.

10-Minute Selection: You can read any selection from this great collection and strike a chord with your young audience. A crowd-pleaser is the hilarious story titled "By Far the Worst Pupil at Long Point School." Uncle Billy stops by for a visit and shares a story about the time his sister—Grandma—was also his teacher. Grandma was always frustrated by the antics of Charlie, the worst student in the small school. The story ends with a surprising tagline.

**Peck, Richard. *The Teacher's Funeral: A Comedy in Three Parts.* Dial, 2004. 190 p.**
Gr. 4–8. Miss Myrt Arbuckle, the teacher of the one-room Hominy Ridge School in rural Indiana, passes away, and the young narrator, Russell, hopes the school year will be canceled. He's horrified to learn that his seventeen-year-old sister, Tansy, has been appointed as the new teacher. This is one of the funniest children's chapter books on the market.

10-Minute Selection: This longish passage is found in chapter 3, "Me and Lloyd and Charlie Parr." Begin with the sentence, "I waited for the right moment: this one." Russell scares his little brother, Lloyd, with a ghost story. Their friend Charlie is in on the prank, which results in Lloyd falling into the creek. Charlie, in turn, falls into the creek in fright when he pulls up a fishing line with a snake on the end. Charlie then tells the brothers about Miss Arbuckle dying. They had to "tie up her jaw with a rag to keep it from sagging." Russell is astounded when he sees a figure approaching the campfire with "her head tied up with a rag." Russell jumps up in fright, steps on a hot coal, and is tossed into the creek. His sister, Tansy, helps pull that trick.

**Pennypacker, Sara. *The Talented Clementine.* Hyperion, 2007. 137 p.**
Gr. K–4. Clementine is worried when all of the third-graders are assigned to perform in a fund-raising talent show called "The Talent-Palooza Night of the Stars!" She doesn't have a talent to share. She takes quick tap-dancing lessons from a girl named Margaret. When Margaret's tap shoes don't fit, Clementine removes the caps from twenty-four bottles of beer with pliers and superglues them to the soles of her sneakers. Clementine's episodes are hilarious, and the actual talent show will have you in tears from laughter, especially when a dozen kids cartwheel right off the stage (onto some padding that Clementine had the foresight to provide). This is the second book in a series about Clementine.

10-Minute Selection: Read chapter 2. Clementine tries to get talent show ideas from the other kids on the school bus. Willy declares he has one talent— stuffing his entire lunch in his mouth at once. "'You do that every day,' I reminded him." Clementine launches into a long story about moving to Egypt because her father might become the new building manager of the pyramids. Her teacher laughs. "There should be a rule about that. No laughing for teachers." Continue reading chapter 4. The kids in Clementine's class describe their talents. Maria's act is "Cartwheel Extravaganza," and she demonstrates by crashing into the chalkboard. Norris's act is "Cartwheel Wham-o-Rama," and he crashes into the hamster cage. "'Now,' my teacher was saying, 'does anyone have an act that *isn't* cartwheeling?' Half the kids put their hands down."

**Perkins, Mitali.** *Rickshaw Girl.* **Charlesbridge, 2007. 91 p.**
Gr. 3–5. Naima is very talented at painting traditional "alpana" designs. "In Naima's village, on International Mother Language Day, when the whole country celebrated the beauty of their Bangla language, the leaders gave a prize to the girl who painted the best alpanas." Naima's father is a rickshaw driver who works long hours. She is worried about her family's financial situation. "'If only I HAD been born a boy,' she thought. 'Then I could earn some money. Even just a little would help!'" Naima eventually learns both how to use her talents and that being female has its advantages.

10-Minute Selection: Read the short fourth and fifth chapters. Naima decides she'll disguise herself and drive her father's rickshaw. She loses control of the rickshaw. It rolls downhill and crashes into a thicket. The leather is scratched, the tin is dented, and the paint is ruined. Skip ahead to chapter 10. Naima is disguised as a boy. She travels to a nearby village to exchange labor for repairs to the rickshaw. She approaches the newly reopened repair shop. She asks an older woman if she could meet with the repairman. The chapter ends with the woman replying, "I *am* the repairman."

**Petty, J. T.** *Clemency Pogue: Fairy Killer.* **Simon and Schuster, 2005. 120 p.**
Gr. 3–6. Clemency is attacked in the woods by a malicious fairy. She saves herself by remembering her childhood stories and yells, "I don't believe in fairies" seven times. The fairy dies, but unfortunately, so do six other fairies—many who are kind and essential to human life, such as the Fairy of Noninvasive Surgery, who was in the process of removing a pea from the ear of a little girl when she was struck down. Accompanied by a hobgoblin, Clemency is off on a worldwide tour to restore the fairies back to life. By doing so, she risks facing, once again, the evil fairy.

10-Minute Selection: Read chapter 2. The evil fairy attacks Clemency. "In its hand it held a wand like a tiny cigarette, dull white all the way up with a searing orange tip, which it thrust into the end of Clemency's nose." The chapter ends with the dead fairy spiraling down into a gorge and Clemency climbing up "onto the safety of the ground just as, near the edge of the woods, the ground, in a mighty soil geyser, exploded."

**Pfeffer, Susan.** *Life as We Knew It.* **Harcourt, 2006. 337 p.**
Gr. 6–12. Life changes for sixteen-year-old Miranda and the entire world after a meteor hits the moon. This causes the moon to alter its orbit around Earth. Tsunamis, earthquakes, volcanoes, and ash covering the sunlight apparently kill

millions of humans. We don't know for sure because we are reading Miranda's diary, and her knowledge is limited to her immediate surroundings. She does know that food, water, and heat are scarce and no one goes to school anymore. When it appears things couldn't get worse, her immediate family is struck down by a potentially lethal flu.

10-Minute Selection: Read most of chapter 2, starting with the line, "The whole school day was just normal." Miranda, her family, and the neighbors watch the meteor strike the moon, but they are soon horrified by a new sight. "It [the moon] was smack in the middle of the sky, way too big, way too visible." Soon, the cell phones stop working, the television signal comes and goes, and reports of widespread tsunamis, caused by the tidal pull of the moon, trickle in. "AP is reporting that Cape Cod . . . has been completely submerged."

**Philbrick, Rodman.** *The Young Man and the Sea.* **Scholastic, 2004. 192 p.**
Gr. 4–7. With a nod to Hemingway, Philbrick relates the story of young Skiff Beaman, whose mother has died. His fisherman father is severely depressed, and their means of income, their boat, *Mary Rose,* has sunk. With the help of a friend, Mr. Woodwell, Skiff raises the boat and sets out to repair it. The story opens with the intriguing sentence, "Before I tell you about the biggest fish in the sea and how it tried to kill me and then ended up saving my life, first you got to know about the leaky boat." Skiff is determined to catch a bluefin tuna that will bring in lots of money for his family. The fish could bring in thousand of dollars. He soon runs into trouble and is alone, miles from shore.

10-Minute Selection: Read the last half of chapter 21, beginning with the sentence, "I'm looking down on the biggest fish I ever seen in my life." Skiff manages to harpoon the fish and in the process is pulled overboard by the fish. Read a few pages into the next chapter, which describes Skiff's thoughts as he's trying hard to hold his breath underwater. End with the sentence "Time to sleep."

**Pratchett, Terry.** *The Amazing Maurice and His Educated Rodents.*
**HarperCollins, 2001. 256 p.**
Gr. 5–10. Maurice is a talking cat in league with a boy named Keith and several rats that also talk and think like humans. They travel from town to town together and pull off a Pied Piper–type scheme. However, they run into trouble in the town of Bad Blintz. Two rat catchers are already at work. The educated rats find a series of traps underground but no local rats. A strange rat king has been created and it is bent on unleashing a rat revenge on mankind. Maurice struggles under the rat king's mind control. There is plenty of action and humor in this, the first Discworld book Pratchett wrote for a younger audience.

10-Minute Selection: Read most of the comical first chapter, beginning with the sentence, "This was the part of the journey the driver didn't like." A stage robber asks a series of Monty Python–like questions of the stagecoach passengers. "Are there any wizards in there?" The bandit also inquires about witches, "heavily armed trolls employed by the mail coach company," werewolves, and vampires. When the highwayman determines it's safe for him to rob the passengers, he finds himself covered with rats and surrenders. End with the sentence, "He wouldn't have hit the ground so hard if someone hadn't tied his bootlaces together." Move on and read the section of chapter 3 where the rats fall into three specialized platoons. Begin with the sentence, "All right, Number Three platoon, you're on widdling duty," and continue until the line, "The Trap Squad trotted away."

**Pratchett, Terry. *The Wee Free Men: A Story of Discworld*. HarperCollins, 2003. 263 p.**
Gr. 5–12. Tiffany Aching is a young witch who is slowly learning about her powers. Tiffany is tested when the evil queen kidnaps her younger brother and takes him into a dreamlike world. Fortunately, Tiffany receives loyal help from the pictsies, also known as the Nac Mac Feegle, or the Wee Free Men. There are hundreds of these six-inch blue warriors who love a good fight. This is one of three Pratchett books that Tiffany appears in.

10-Minute Selection: Read the middle section of chapter 3, "Hunt the Hag." Begin with the sentence, "There was only one place where it was possible for someone in a large family to be private, and that was in the privy." Tiffany first encounters the Wee Free Men. They steal one of her sheep. She next catches two of them in the act stealing eggs from the henhouse. End with the line, "And she thought: I think I need a whole egg's worth of education, in a hurry." Read one more brief selection, from the middle of chapter 7, "First Sight and Second Thoughts." Tiffany has a hilarious exchange with the Wee Free Man known as No'-as-big-as-Medium-Sized-Jock-but-bigger-than-Wee-Jock-Jock. Begin with the sentence, "What's your name, pictsie?" and finish with "'There's been many a fine story o' the exploits o' No'-as-big-as-Medium-Sized-Jock-but-bigger-than-Wee-Jock-Jock,' the pictsie added, looking so earnest that Tiffany didn't have the heart to say that they must have been very long stories."

**Pullman, Philip. *I Was a Rat!* Knopf, 2000. 165 p.**
Gr. 3–6. A little boy shows up at the house of a poor cobbler and washerwoman and tells them, "I was a rat." He tells the couple that he's three weeks old. Bob and Joan name him Roger and try to help the boy. "Well, we got to do what's right. There's clever folks in the City Hall, they know what's right." However, the lady at City Hall is no help. Neither is the orphanage, the police, the hospital, the school, or even the Philosopher Royal. Roger runs away, only to get stuck first in a traveling carnival and then with some boy thieves. The whole time, Bob and Joan

search for Roger, who heads for the sewers. It takes a character from a popular fairy tale to solve the mystery of the boy who claimed to have once been a rat.

10-Minute Selection: Read the first chapter, "I Was a Rat!" Bob and Joan try to feed the boy, who is unfamiliar with utensils. They name him Roger and theorize. "He's a wild boy, and he was brung up by rats." Move on to the chapter titled "School." Bob and Joan take Roger to school. The mean Mrs. Cribbin raises her hand, and "Roger, seeing a threat, leapt up to bite her hand. He got a good mouthful of it and shook hard." Roger gets sent to the headmaster to be caned. The chapter ends with Roger making his escape.

**Pullman, Philip. *The Scarecrow and His Servant.* Knopf, 2004. 229 p.**
Gr. 3–6. A scarecrow with a turnip for a head comes alive when lightning strikes him. An orphaned boy named Jack witnesses the event and accepts the offer to be the scarecrow's servant. The two seek adventures, which include scaring a gang of thieving brigands, joining a theater troupe, fighting in a war, and becoming marooned on an island. They are saved by birds that have convened on the island for "The Eighty-Four Thousand Five Hundred and Seventy-Eighth Grand Congress of All Birds." The scarecrow, Jack, and the birds join forces to rid Spring Valley of poisonous factories. The dialogue of all characters is a delight to read aloud, particularly the scarecrow's combination of innocence and sophistication: "Well, that obviously means that hostilities are suspended until they hatch. . . . You birds in there, in view of your impending parenthood, I shall not scare you away."

10-Minute Selection: Read chapter 3. Jack and the scarecrow are hiding in the brigands' headquarters. When Jack is found, he quickly gathers his wits and entertains the robbers with a ghost story about a dead man who wouldn't stay buried. At this point, the scarecrow rises from his hiding place and scares the brigands away. Finish with the line, "So Jack took the bag of food he'd hidden earlier and added a pie and a cold roast chicken for good measure, then followed his master out onto the high road, which was shining bright under the moon."

**Rallison, Janette. *All's Fair in Love, War, and High School.* Walker, 2003. 202 p.**
Gr. 7–10. Samantha is a very popular cheerleader who appears to have the perfect life. However, she learns that her SAT scores are very low, jeopardizing her chances to attend college. Then her boyfriend breaks up with her, leaving her without a date to the prom. She decides to run for student-body president to make up for her poor test scores. She is challenged by her ex-boyfriend, Logan, to control her sharp tongue and tries to go for two weeks without insulting anyone.

10-Minute Selection: Read the last section of chapter 1. Samantha creates an imaginary conversation with her parents when they learn about her SAT scores. Next, read chapter 2. Samantha's mom forces her to drop the family cat off at the vet's (to be spayed), while Samantha is on a date. Her date obviously doesn't care for cats, especially cats that threaten to throw up in his car. "Who knows what that psycho cat of yours did underneath the seat." The highlight of the chapter is when the cat climbs on top of Samantha's head, while still in the car, and a group of teenage boys drive past. "[A]ll of them stared openmouthed at me. Their mouths were open, I assume, because they were laughing too hard to shut them."

**Resau, Laura.** *Red Glass.* **Delacorte, 2007. 275 p.**
Gr. 9–12. Sophie and her family take care of a six-year-old boy named Pablo whose family died crossing the border into Arizona. They locate the rest of Pablo's family in Mexico. Sophie and her aunt Dika take Pablo to meet his relatives. Dika's boyfriend, Mr. Lorenzo, and his teenage son, Angel, who plan to travel further into Guatemala, accompany them. Sophie, who is fragile and constantly worried about things, is exposed to new hardships and learns about strength and love. This emotional, beautifully written book has many Spanish phrases scattered throughout the text.

10-Minute Selection: Read the first few pages of chapter 2, "Midnight Parties." Sophie recalls a tender memory of her family helping poor, desperate Mexicans in the middle of the night. Finish with the sentence, "As I got older, they reminded me of what mattered in life." Pick up with a suspenseful scene in chapter 16, "Unforeseen Journey." Sophie takes a dangerous solo trip from southern Mexico to Guatemala to find Angel and his father. Start with the sentence, "The slimy-friendly guy moved next to me," and continue to the line, "That was when a group of five guys came out of the shadows and swaggered toward us."

**Riordan, Rick.** *The Lightning Thief.* **Hyperion, 2005. 375 p.**
Gr. 4–9. This first book of the Percy Jackson and the Olympians series introduces us to young Percy, a twelve-year-old who bounces from one boarding school to another. After a series of weird and dangerous adventures, Percy learns that his father is the immortal Poseidon, Greek god of the sea. He also learns that he's angered some of the other gods of Mount Olympus; he's accused of stealing Zeus's lightning bolt. Percy and his friends must find the real thief before they are killed.

10-Minute Selection: Read chapter 1, "I Accidentally Vaporize My Pre-Algebra Teacher." Percy and his classmates are on a field trip when his teacher, Mrs. Dodds, turns into "a shriveled hag with bat wings and claws and a mouth full of yellow fangs" and attacks him. Read a portion of chapter 2, in which Percy overhears a conversation between Mr. Brunner and a satyr named Grover. Begin with the sentence that starts, "The evening before my final . . ." and continue until the line, "They thought I was in some kind of danger."

Second 10-Minute Selection: Read chapter 4, "My Mother Teaches Me Bullfighting." The Minotaur attacks Percy, his mother, and Grover. "But I just stood there, frozen in fear, as the monster charged her. She tried to sidestep, as she'd told me to do, but the monster learned his lesson. His hand shot out and grabbed her by the neck as she tried to get away."

**Ritter, John H. *The Boy Who Saved Baseball.* Philomel, 2003. 216 p.**
Gr. 5–7. A legendary baseball field is in danger of being destroyed by developers unless a coed team of nine kids can defeat an all-star team of twelve-year-olds. Help comes unexpectedly: first, by a horse-riding kid named Cruz de la Cruz, who thinks he has almost solved the mystery of hitting a baseball, and second, in the form of Dante Del Gato, an ex-baseball player who may have actually discovered the secret of perfect batting.

10-Minute Selection: Start reading in chapter 12 with the sentences, "De Gato waved everyone close. 'Look, I'm not a coach,'" and read until the end of the chapter. Begin again with chapter 13, starting with the sentence, "After lunch, Tom's dad assembled the team in the dugout and announced a new strategy," and continue until the end of the chapter. Del Gato takes over as the new coach and has the kids performing unusual drills, such as hitting against Maria, who pitches underhand, and running down a mountainside as fast as they can.

**Roberts, Diane. *Made You Look.* Delacorte, 2003. 150 p.**
Gr. 4–6. This story features a game show similar to those found on the Nickelodeon network. Jason dreams of appearing on the popular kids' show *Masquerade Mania*. His dream has a chance of coming true when his father promises to bring the whole family from Texas to California. Unfortunately, they're not flying. They are traveling as a family in "a prehistoric camper that looks like a giant sardine can." Jason is not thrilled to travel with his two sisters, either.

10-Minute Selection: Start right off by reading the first chapter in its entirety. The author does a nice job setting the scenario quickly. She also gives a good description of the wackiness involved with the game show. Contestants must perform crazy stunts if they land on "a WHOOPS!" They may have buckets of slimy spaghetti fall on them or be pelted by water balloons or covered in chocolate syrup. If they win, however, they could get cool prizes. "Once I saw a kid win an Xbox and a year's supply of video games and he passed out cold."

**Ryan, Pam Muñoz. *Becoming Naomi León.* Scholastic, 2004. 246 p.**
Gr. 4–7. Naomi and her younger brother, Owen, are content with their life with Gram after their mother, Skyla, abandoned the two of them years ago. Now Skyla is back, threatening to take Naomi for the child-support money. The tension builds as Naomi and the reader slowly learn how mean and calculating Skyla is. Gram takes action and hides Naomi and Owen in Mexico to search for the children's birth father.

10-Minute Selection: Read most of chapter 10, "A Schizophrenia of Hawks." Start with the sentence, "'We have a problem,' said Gram, rushing into the trailer on Thursday afternoon," and read until the end of the chapter. Skyla volunteers to take Owen, who has physical problems from birth defects, to the Children's Hospital for his appointment. "Besides, I *am* his mother." Skyla loses her temper at the doctors and then the kids. She slaps Naomi after they return to Gram's trailer and then makes a veiled threat about Gram. "You know, if anything happens to Gram, all you'll have is me anyway, and something could happen to her any time now, old as she is."

**Ryan, Pam Muñoz. *Esperanza Rising*. Scholastic, 2000. 262 p.**
Gr. 5–8. Esperanza's father, a wealthy landowner in Mexico, is murdered. The fourteen-year-old Esperanza, her mother, their housekeeper Hortensia, and her son Miguel flee to the United States. Esperanza is not used to hard labor and has a tough time adjusting to migrant-camp conditions. She eventually learns to help others. The story is based on experiences of Ryan's grandmother. There are many Spanish terms woven into the text.

10-Minute Selection: Read one of two selections (or both) from the chapter titled "Las Guayabas: Guavas." The first selection starts with the sentence, "The locomotive arrived pulling a line of cars hissing and spewing steam." Esperanza doesn't want anything to do with the peasants riding in the train car for the poor with her. She makes a little girl cry and eventually helps her mother make a doll for the child. Finish with the line, "Otherwise, she would have been reminded of her own selfishness and Mama's disapproval for miles to come."

Second 10-Minute Selection: In the same chapter is a passage that features an encounter between Esperanza and a poor woman. Begin with the sentence, "They had been on the train for four days and nights when a woman got on with a wire cage containing six red hens." Esperanza is surprised when Miguel points out some differences between the rich and the poor. She refutes one of his observations as "something that old wives say." End the passage with his response: "It is something the poor say."

**Ryan, Pam Muñoz. *Paint the Wind*. Scholastic, 2007. 336 p.**
Gr. 4–6. Orphan Maya leaves California and goes to live with her relatives on a Wyoming ranch and field camp. Maya was unaware of their existence even though she was supposed to spend every summer with them. Her grandmother, who had just passed away, secretly kept Maya from her maternal grandfather, Moose; her great-uncle Fig; her great-aunt Violet; and her pesky cousin Payton. They watch wild horses, including the mare Artemisia and her foal, Klee. Later, Maya goes down into a gorge by herself to search for the horses. With little warning, an earthquake hits.

10-Minute Selection: Read the entire chapter 21. Maya is hurtled from her horse, Seltzer, when the earthquake strikes. Seltzer runs away. Maya finds Artemisia and Klee in danger. "Maya lunged toward a tree trunk to steady herself and heard rubble sliding from the hillside above. She spun around to see a waterfall of rocks descending on Klee, entombing him." Finish the chapter and skip ahead to the first three pages of chapter 24. Maya tries to determine how long she has been surviving in the outdoors. "Was it five days or six . . . or more?" She has little strength. Her sleep is interrupted when she "awoke to a strange cry, like the wail of a newborn baby." End with the sentence, "A mountain lion."

**Sachar, Louis. *Small Steps.* Delacorte, 2006. 257 p.**
Gr. 5–8. Armpit is trying to get his life straightened out. He's doing his best to take small steps with his goals. "1. Graduate from high school. 2. Get a job. 3. Save his money. 4. Avoid situations that might turn violent. And 5. Lose the name Armpit." His ex–Camp Green Lake companion X-Ray threatens to ruin Armpit's goals with a get-rich-quick concert-ticket scheme. Armpit winds up taking his ten-year-old neighbor, Ginny, to popular teen sensation Kaira DeLeon's music concert. Armpit actually meets Kaira, and the two hit it off. Armpit also becomes entangled in a murder attempt on Kaira's life. He's being set up to take the blame. This is the companion book to Sachar's award-winning title *Holes*.

10-Minute Selection: Tell your audience that anyone who has read Louis Sachar's *Holes* might remember the characters Armpit and X-Ray. Inform them that Armpit is trying to turn his life around, and he's taking his neighbor Ginny to a pop concert. Read chapter 15, where the two are at the concert. Security guards tackle Armpit because of his counterfeit tickets. This causes Ginny to go into a cerebral palsy seizure. Kaira is informed about the disturbance in the audience and invites Ginny and Armpit to watch the concert backstage.

**Sage, Angie. *My Haunted House.* HarperCollins, 2006. 133 p.**
Gr. 1–4. The first book in the Araminta Spookie series introduces us to Araminta, her aunt Tabby, and her uncle Drac. Tabby is tired of battling the boiler and de-cides to sell their eclectic house. Araminta does everything she can to sabotage the plan. She finds and enlists two ghosts, discovers the secret entrance to a bal-cony, and executes her Awful Ambush, which includes dropping bats, spiders, and Extra-Sticky Strawberry Jell-O on the heads of potential buyers. Young children will enjoy this silly ghost story.

10-Minute Selection: Read chapter 2, "This House Is For Sale." Araminta throws the contents of a very old fish bowl ("it was full of slime, old weeds, and some very smelly green water") on the head of a real-estate agent. She also rewrites Tabby's sign to read "This House Is Not For Sale." Continue reading chapter 2, "Huge Hotels." Araminta launches her Ghost Kit at a woman who is thinking of converting the home into a hotel. The woman goes "straight through one of the oldest cobwebs, where the biggest, hairiest spiders live—and I saw the biggest, hairiest spider of them all fall down her front."

**Salisbury, Graham.** *Eyes of the Emperor.* **Wendy Lamb, 2005. 229 p.**
Gr. 6–10. Eddy Okubo is a Japanese American boy who lies about his age to enlist in the U.S. Army shortly after the attack on Pearl Harbor. The racism that he and his friends face from the military escalates until the Japanese American soldiers are ordered to take part in a terrifying experiment. They are taken to Cat Island, in the Mississippi Sound, where they are to be the "bait" in what turns out to be an unsuccessful attempt to train dogs to sniff out people of Japanese ancestry. According to the author's notes, the story is based on true events.

10-Minute Selection: Read chapter 28, "Kooch." Eddy meets the dog that will be tracking him in the wilderness. He is told to hide but is also warned to watch out for snakes, gators, boars, and scorpions. The first stage of this experiment is for Eddy to lie down and place a bag of horsemeat on his throat. "The dog's going to come up and eat it off you, right there under your chin." Continue reading the next two short chapters. The Japanese Americans are puzzled about the experiment. Chapter 30 ends with a disgusted Eddy thinking, "I'd thought we would be treated like real soldiers. But no. Not us."

**Salisbury, Graham.** *Night of the Howling Dogs.* **Wendy Lamb, 2007. 191 p.**
Gr. 4–8. A Hawaiian Boy Scout troop camps along a remote section of the coast under the shadow of the Kilauea volcano. Senior patrol leader Dylan doesn't get along with Louie, a tough kid whom Mr. Bellows, the scout leader, has befriended. While camping, Dylan sees two wild dogs. Some cowboys who have come to the coast to fish join the troop. One of the cowboys, Masa, believes that the white wild dog is the spirit of Pele, a Hawaiian legend, roaming the area to warn the campers. Everyone's life is in danger when an earthquake sends boulders on Dylan's shelter and then triggers a tsunami. Dylan and Louie must work together to save the others. Share the author's note in the back matter. This fictionalized story was based on a similar, real-life scouting trip that the author's cousin experienced. The story contains a few Hawaiian words.

10-Minute Selection: Read chapter 11, "The Heat Equation." The two adult scout leaders and the younger scouts leave the camp for a hike. Casey, Mike, narrator Dylan, and his nemesis, Louie, stay behind. Dylan learns a little more of Louie's rough background. The chapter ends with Louie asking Dylan, "You like go round with me punk?" Continue reading chapter 12, "The Shark." The four boys swim out to an island and notice a shark is following them. Louie proves he's tough by swimming near the shark.

**Schmidt, Gary D. *The Wednesday Wars*. Clarion, 2007. 264 p.**
Gr. 4–8. It's 1967. The Vietnam War is in the background but on everyone's mind. At the Camillo Junior High, half of the seventh-graders leave class each Wednesday afternoon for catechism. The other half attends Hebrew school. That leaves Holling Hoodhood, a Presbyterian, all alone with his teacher, Mrs. Baker. She has him do chores for a few weeks before deciding their time will be better spent reading Shakespeare. Holling is surprised to discover that he enjoys Shakespeare, although this new knowledge lands him a role in a play that requires him to wear yellow tights with white feathers. Other memorable scenes include visits from some New York Yankees, a track race, a school camping trip, a heroic bus misadventure, a runaway sister, and two escaped pet rats.

10-Minute Selection: Read the beginning of the chapter titled "November" through to the sentence, "'Thanks,' he said, and ran ahead, the scent of cigarette smoke lingering in the air." Holling loves the way the character Caliban swears in *The Tempest*. Holling practices several phrases, such as "The red plague rid you," "apes with foreheads villainous low," and "pied ninny." His classmate Meryl Lee insults him during chorus, and Holling responds with, "Blind mole, a wicked dew from unwholesome fen drop you."

**Schwartz, Virginia Frances. *4 Kids in 5E and 1 Crazy Year*. Holiday House, 2006. 265 p.**
Gr. 4–5. PS 1 in Queens is overcrowded; four fifth-grade classes are not enough. The teachers and school officials pull a few students from each section to create a fifth class. Four students from 5E—Giovanni, Destiny, Willie, and Maximo—take turns telling stories about themselves, their classmates, and their teacher. Ms. Hill inspires the kids to draw upon their own lives to create stories and poems. By the end of the school year, the class is excited about entering a writing contest.

10-Minute Selection: The chapters are grouped by the months of the school year. Read the first October chapter, "We're In But I'm Out," featuring Maximo. Ms. Hill teaches the students to write about place. Maximo struggles with the assignment. "How can I tell anybody I lived in a shelter for abused women, under a court order of protection?" Skip ahead to the January chapter featuring Giovanni, "No Problems Please." Giovanni is worried that he will be held back because he can't read well. He's inspired by Gary Paulsen's book *Hatchet*. He asks Max to take him to the public library. "[T]he librarian hands me my first ever library card. . . . When I sign my name on the back, I feel rich. Suddenly, I am someone who reads."

**Scieszka, Jon. *See You Later, Gladiator*. Viking, 2000. 85 p.**
Gr. 1–4. The Time Warp Trio—Joe, Sam, and Fred—are wrestling when they knock a bookcase over, and the Book, their time-traveling artifact, delivers them

to an ancient Roman gladiator school. They meet a slave called the Professor, who tries to help them recover the Book and return to their own time. They are all loaded on a cart and delivered to the Colosseum to do battle before the emperor. They use tactics from modern-day professional wrestling to escape. "We call it the Time Warp Trio Blind Ninja Smackdown." This is one of many books in the very popular Time Warp Trio series.

10-Minute Selection: Read chapter 4. The boys find a food hall and join several fighters for a meal. Sam gets into a belching display with a gladiator. Move to the end of chapter 5 with the sentence, "I could take any of these guys and throw him and pin him and—," where Fred accidentally tosses "a sloppy handful of chicken crud" on a nasty gladiator named Horridus. Continue reading chapter 6. Joe outwits Horridus and another gladiator named Brutus. If time permits, read chapter 7, where the boys' battle with Horridus and Brutus turns into a classic food fight.

**Shahan, Sherry. *Death Mountain*. Peachtree, 2005. 202 p.**
Gr. 5–8. Two teenage girls, Erin and Mae, virtual strangers, are caught in a fierce electrical storm and find themselves lost in the Sierra Nevada Mountains. Erin has a fair amount of experience in the wilderness, but both girls must work together to find food and protect themselves from the elements. Along the way, they learn more about each other and themselves.

10-Minute Selection: Read chapter 6, where the girls get separated from their wilderness-survival group during the storm. The group is exposed to lightning on a ridge. Mae panics and sets off running. Mae's brother, Levi, injures his ankle and hollers for Erin to follow her. Erin sees what she thinks is a bear. The chapter ends with Erin still shouting out Mae's name. Continue reading the very short chapter 10. The girls hear a noise in the middle of the night. Erin assures Mae that it's only coyotes. They hear scratching closer to their tents. "Erin listened. 'Raccoons forage along rivers. Maybe we moved into a den.' 'They're vegetarians, right?' Mae sounded scared." End the selection with the following passage: "Another branch cracked. The girls strained to listen. Suddenly, something large and furry burst into the shelter."

**Shalant, Phyllis. *The Great Cape Rescue*. Dutton, 2007. 128 p.**
Gr. 4–5. Four boys entering fourth grade love to pretend they are superheroes. They worry that kids will laugh at them for their "babyish" activities, so they try to keep their exploits quiet. The story focuses on Finch, who discovers that his pretend superhero cape is actually a magical Thinking Cape. The cape communicates with all four friends through telepathy. The friends learn to band together when dealing with the school bully, Thorn, and his followers. Problems arise when the Thinking Cape goes missing. This fantasy is the first in the Society of Super Secret Heroes series.

10-Minute Selection: Before you read the selection, tell the audience that Finch has discovered that his superhero cape is magical and they communicate telepathically. Start with a few pages in chapter 12, "Cornered," with the sentence, "Finch reached into his bag for his math book and felt the soft cloth of the Thinking Cape." Read until the end of the chapter. Finch is trapped in the boys' bathroom with the bully, Thorn. The Thinking Cape helps Finch delay the fight. Read the entire next chapter, "To Punch or Not to Punch." Finch meets Thorn outside for a fight. Finch unpacks first-aid supplies and tells Thorn that they're for him. Thorn retreats when the other three members of the Society of Super Secret Heroes show up. The Thinking Cape's dialogue is italicized throughout the text. Read these lines in a hushed, steady voice.

**Shusterman, Neal. *Dread Locks*. Dutton, 2005. 164 p.**
Gr. 7–10. Who or what is the mysterious new high school girl Tara? She always wears dark glasses, and she lives alone in a mansion that holds many statues. One by one, she turns her attention to different students, and their behavior changes. Her neighbor, fifteen-year-old Parker Baer, who Tara calls Baby Baer, becomes her accomplice and starts changing, too. Shusterman combines the folktale "Goldilocks and the Three Bears" with the Greek legends of Medusa in this thriller. This book is one of the Dark Fusion series.

10-Minute Selection: Read the beginning third and last third of chapter 9, "The First Lock." The first section finds Parker introducing Tara to his older brother, Garrett. Parker and Garrett just had a nasty fight. Tara wants to help Parker get revenge and convinces Garrett to taker her out on a date. Stop at the line, "It now hung in a tightly wound auburn curl." Pick up your reading in the same chapter with the sentence, "I went home and just sat in my room in the dark." Finish the chapter. Garrett returns from his date with Tara, and he has little recollection of the evening. He tells Parker that he only remembers one thing: "She took off her glasses."

**Shusterman, Neal. *Unwind*. Simon and Schuster, 2007. 335 p.**
Gr. 6–12. This amazing book will foster hours of discussion among young people. In the future, teens may be "unwound," or harvested for their organs, by their parents or, in the case of orphan Risa, the state. She is running away from the Juvey-cops with Connor, whose parents signed him over for unwinding, and Lev, who was raised as a tithe, a sacrifice by his parents. They meet other "Unwinds" while being smuggled to the Graveyard, led by the Admiral, who once had his own son harvested.

10-Minute Selection: Read "The Bill of Life," listed before the first chapter. It briefly describes the Second Civil War, which led to a compromise between the Pro-Life and Pro-Choice armies. "Human life may not be touched from the moment of conception until a child reaches the age of thirteen." A parent may "choose to retroactively 'abort' a child." Read chapter 1, which features Connor. Connor is shocked to learn that his parents have signed the Unwind order. He runs away and hides in a truck stop and meets a sympathetic truck driver who hides him aboard. Hours later, Connor hears "Come on out, kid. Your ride's over." It's not the truck driver—it's the police with his father, who used Connor's cell phone to locate him. Connor takes off, with tranquilizer bullets flying by him. A car swerves to avoid him and crashes. The chapter ends with Connor reaching in to grab the kid in the car.

**Smelcer, John. *The Trap*. Holt, 2006. 170 p.**
Gr. 6–12. Albert Least-Weasel, who has been trapping in the north woods for decades, gets his leg caught in one of his traps. His snowmobile and his supplies are just out of reach, and it is the middle of winter. He quickly prepares himself against both the bitter cold and a pack of hungry wolves that are roaming nearby. The story is told in alternate chapters following both Albert and his teenage grandson Johnny. Johnny is the only one who worries about his grandfather. He is told, "He has been going out there to that trapline since you daddy born. He don't need you or nobody when he go out there. Someday you learn that, Johnny." Despite what others say, Johnny sets off in search of his missing grandfather.

10-Minute Selection: Start a few pages into the book with the sentence, "Rounding the last turn, disappearing for a minute and then coming into view again, the snowmobile dragged itself and its sled up to a stand of trees and stopped." Read to the end of the chapter. Albert is studying his trap when "there was a soft click as the teeth of steel closed on his leg."

**Smith, D. James. *The Boys of San Joaquin*. Atheneum, 2005. 231 p.**
Gr. 5–8. The year is 1951, and the location is Orange Grove City, California. Twelve-year-old Paolo finds his dog with a twenty-dollar bill in its mouth. He sets out to discover where this treasure must be buried, and along the way, he discovers that money from the local church is missing. The sequel is titled *Probably the World's Best Story about a Dog and the Girl Who Loved Me*.

10-Minute Selection: Start near the beginning of the book with the line, "Rufus—he was the dog—comes around one summer morning after a night out sporting, and he's got a twenty-dollar bill, half-shredded, sticking out of his teeth." Finish the rest of the first chapter, and continue into the second chapter, when Paolo and his deaf cousin, Billy, encourage Rufus to show them where he found the money. They wind up in the monsignor's garden at the Cathedral of San Joaquin and are confronted by the rough caretaker, Early Johnson. The chapter ends with the sentence, "Rufus has a face full of mud, and Billy is waving what looks like might be a five-dollar bill."

**Smith, Roland.** *Peak.* **Harcourt, 2007. 246 p.**
Gr. 4–10. Peak Marcello is the son of two experienced mountain climbers. He has been caught illegally climbing a skyscraper. Another boy tries to duplicate his feat and dies. Peak is fined and sent out of town. His father, who is leading a team up Mount Everest, has plans for Peak to become the youngest climber to reach the summit. On the way, Peak makes a great sacrifice.

10-Minute Selection: Read the second chapter, "The Hook." Peak is climbing when the weather turns bad. His right ear and cheek get frozen to the wall. "To reach the top you must have resolve, muscles, skills and . . . A FACE!" As he reaches the top, we learn that Peak has been climbing a skyscraper, not a mountain, and that the police are waiting at the top for him. Next, read the second half of the chapter titled "ABC." Peak is with other climbers and a film crew. They are trying to reach ABC, which stands for Advance Base Camp. "ABC: 21,161 feet. Higher than Kilimanjaro and Mount McKinley." Begin with the sentence, "At midmorning the weather turned, with gray clouds coming in from the west and a bitterly cold wind blowing down the mountains," and read until the end of the chapter. The climb is rough for everyone. Zopa's words echo in Peak's brain: "You can never tell who the mountain will allow and who it will not."

**Soto, Gary.** *Afterlife.* **Harcourt, 2003. 158 p.**
Gr. 6–12. Seventeen-year-old Chuy walks into a club's men's room, tells a guy he likes his shoes, and is stabbed for it. "The guy next to me, the one with the yellow shoes, worked an arm around my throat, snakelike, and with his free hand plunged a knife into my chest. . . . 'What did you say to me, *cabrón?*' he breathed in my ear." Chuy's ghost visits his family, finds his killer, and roams his city. He meets Crystal, a recent suicide, and Robert, a homeless man lately dead.

10-Minute Selection: Read chapter 3. Chuy spots his murderer, "the dude with the yellow shoes." Chuy is able to freak out his killer by breathing on him. He then thrusts his hand inside the guy to "let him feel the coldness of a ghostly fist." The killer meets up with another rough kid, whom Chuy recognizes from middle school. The two bad boys get into a fight, and Chuy decides to leave. "I could always hunt Yellow Shoes later. . . . I winced when I heard a scream coming from the house. Someone was hurting . . ." End with the sentence, "It wasn't anyone decent, just two thugs heading for an early grave."

**Soto, Gary.** *Worlds Apart: Traveling with Fernie and Me.* **Putnam, 2005. 56 p.**
Gr. 4–6. This very short novel-in-verse follows two boys as they travel around the world. They start out visiting San Francisco and then take an ocean liner to Hawaii. By the time their travels are over, they have stopped in Australia, Asia, Africa, Europe, and most of the Western Hemisphere before hitchhiking in Arizona. To their surprise, they are picked up by their teacher, and we learn that their trip

took place in their imaginations. This is the sequel to *Fearless Fernie: Hanging Out with Fernie and Me.*

   10-Minute Selection: Pick and choose several of your favorite poems to read aloud. Or read a poem a day for several days and mark the boys' progress with a globe. Begin with the first poem, "Itching to Travel," in which they first start out, daring their shadows to keep up with them. My favorite is "Tattoos," where the boys are covered with tattoos, even inside their ears and on their tongues. The tattoos are the stick-on type, and when the boys go swimming, the tattoos wash off: "Where, I like to think, one or two attached themselves / To the fins of two bright but goofy fish."

**Spinelli, Jerry. *Stargirl*. Knopf, 2000. 176 p.**
Gr. 6–10. The students of Mica High School are fascinated with the nonconform-ist behavior of a new student known as Stargirl. She dresses in outrageous outfits, such as a kimono or a 1920s flapper dress. Her popularity soon reverses when she starts cheering for both teams at basketball games and refuses to recognize the op-ponents as the enemy. "At that point the only crime Stargirl could have been accused of would be corniness. But she didn't stop there. She cheered whenever a ball went in, regardless of which team shot it. . . . At first the other cheerleaders tried to suppress her; it was like trying to calm down a puppy." The sequel is titled *Love, Stargirl.*

   10-Minute Selection: Read the first two chapters in their entirety. The first chapter opens with the line, "Did you see her?" Stargirl strums a ukulele and sings in the school cafeteria. "Heads swung, eyes followed her, mouths hung open. Disbelief." Chapter 2 opens with a student named Hillari declaring that Stargirl is not real. "She's an actress. It's a scam." Stargirl dresses in wild outfits the rest of the month. She serenades people on their birthdays. She makes up songs about isosceles triangles. She even dances outside in the rain during gym class. Some students suspect she's not a real student, but the narrator knows, "Stargirl *was* real."

**Springer, Nancy, ed. *Ribbiting Tales: Original Stories about Frogs*. Philomel, 2000. 112 p.**
Gr. 3–5. Highlights in this collection of eight frog stories include "A Boy and His Frog," by David Lubar; "It Came from Outer Little Pond," by Brian Jacques, in which a tiny frog saves the frog kingdom from a powerful blue frog (we later learn the blue frog is a children's battery-powered toy); "Ahem," by Nancy Springer, in which a girl literally has a frog in her throat that helps her overcome her shyness; "In the Frog King's Court," by Bruce Coville, in which a boy named Dennis learns that he is part frog (his great-uncle Hopgo was kissed by a princess years ago and turned into a human); and Jane Yolen's version of "The Pied Piper of Hamelin," titled "Green Plague."

10-Minute Selection: Read Lubar's story, about a boy whose pet frog, Jumpy, gets bigger and bigger. It eventually eats one of the neighbor's annoying Chihuahuas. "He just sat there calmly for a moment, then he flicked out his tongue and snatched one of the dogs. Slurp." The boy takes Jumpy to a nearby swamp. Two years later, stories emerge about disappearing wildlife near the swamp. The boy decides to raise oversized flies to take to the swamp. He succeeds—and the first overgrown fly is called Buzzella. "In a month, she was as large as a vulture. I kept her in an old birdcage."

**Staples, Suzanne Fisher.** *The Green Dog.* **Farrar Straus Giroux, 2003. 120 p.**
Gr. 3–5. Suzanne wants a dog. One shows up in her life, and she names him Jeff. Jeff gets into trouble. He digs up a neighbor's garden. He knocks a can of green paint over himself, hence the book's title. The story is loosely based on the author's life. Listeners might feel the story ends too abruptly until they realize a doctor's parting words are about the protagonist. "She has an active imagination, and that might turn out to be a good thing someday."

10-Minute Selection: Read the end of the first chapter, "Girl Needs Dog," starting with the sentence, "I reach the creek (which we pronounce 'crick') that bounces in silvery riffles over rocks and fallen tree limbs down to the lake." Suzanne finds several tadpoles. Continue reading into the next chapter, "Dogless Days." Suzanne temporarily stores the tadpoles in the toilet, but someone flushes them. End with the sentence, "I put my head down and race off toward the creek." Next, read a passage from the chapter titled "Dog in Danger," beginning with the line, "It's a hot summer day, and the air seems to shimmer above the surface of Route 6." The whole family sees a dog in the road with cars whizzing past. Suzanne's father keeps driving. End with "I am stunned." Skip over and read the first two pages of the next chapter, "A Small Miracle." The family is surprised to find the dog at their place. End with the line, "Nobody seems to have any problem with his name."

**Stewart, Trenton Lee.** *The Mysterious Benedict Society.* **Little, Brown, 2007. 486 p.**
Gr. 4–7. Reynie Muldoon, an extremely smart orphan, answers an ad that reads, "ARE YOU A GIFTED CHILD LOOKING FOR SPECIAL OPPORTUNITIES?" He takes a series of tests and finds himself grouped with three other extraordinary children: the nervous George "Sticky" Washington, the acrobatic Kate Wetherall, and the cranky Constance Contraire. They form a group of spies for Mr. Benedict, who has learned that the Learning Institute for the Very Enlightened is actually a front for a mysterious madman who is trying to control the world through mind domination. The sequel is titled *The Mysterious Benedict Society and the Perilous Journey.*

10-Minute Selection: Read the last portion of the first chapter, where Reynie and several other children are taking a test. Some of the children burst into tears and flee the room upon seeing the first question. Begin with the line, "Inside the Monk Building, conspicuously posted signs led them down a series of corridors, past a room where a handful of parents waited anxiously, and at last into a room crowded with children in desks," and read until the end of the chapter. Some of the test questions are challenging to read aloud. "The fourth question asked which church was built by the emperor Justinian to demonstrate his superiority to the late Theodoric's Ostrogothic successors." However, your audience will enjoy hearing how Reynie figures out the answers. At the end of the chapter, the test giver states, "'I shall read now the names of those who passed the test . . . Reynard Muldoon!' . . . On her way out of the room, she added, 'That is all.'"

**Thomas, Jane Resh.** *Blind Mountain.* **Clarion, 2006. 117 p.**
Gr. 4–6. Eleven-year-old Sam accidentally blinds his overbearing surgeon father with a pine branch while the two are mountain climbing in Montana. Dad's cornea is scratched, and there's danger of infection. Since they had only planned for a day trip, they don't have any camping supplies. Sam must successfully navigate his father and their dog, Mac, down the mountainside. The two constantly argue. "Numbskull! Are you stupid, Sam? I've told you a million times . . ." During the night, they realize that a wounded cougar is stalking them. His father believes Sam has a knife and hatchet, but Sam has lost the hatchet. "No weapon at all except his jackknife. The Swiss Army knife's corkscrews and screwdrivers were useless."

10-Minute Selection: Read the last two paragraphs of the first chapter, when Sam releases the branch. "His father was on his knees and under one tree, clutching his face and swearing. 'Bloody branch caught me right across the eyes,' he groaned. 'Never saw it coming.'" Continue reading into the second chapter up to the line, "How would Sam find the way down?" Skip ahead and read all of chapter 6. Sam wakes up and sees the cougar for the first time. They realize the cougar is wounded. "'We're slower than other game.' Other game. They were prey." The cougar disappears, but Sam is worried because dawn is still six hours away.

**Van Draanen, Wendelin.** *Sammy Keyes and the Wild Things.* **Knopf, 2007. 293 p.**
Gr. 4–8. Sammy Keyes gets talked into a hiking trip with her classmate Cricket to look for condors. Cricket belongs to a scout troop of three girls dedicated to monitoring the birds. They find an injured condor they name Marvin; the bird has been shot. The kids also learn that Marvin's mother, Big Mama, is missing. Sammy follows a series of clues that point to an elaborate poaching scheme to illegally sell a condor to an international bird collector. This is one of several Sammy Keyes mystery books.

10-Minute Selection: Read chapter 6. Cricket is helping Sammy learn about camping and the great outdoors. Sammy is concerned to hear about ticks, scorpions, and mosquitoes. The passage turns hilarious "when one of those pesky little flies shoots right up my nose." Sammy tries to snort it out, but it won't budge. She panics and yells. Her echo intrigues the other girls, who start shouting into the canyon to hear their echoes. Sammy finally sucks it up, and "I rasp it forward and hock a big ol' fly loogie onto the ground."

**Vernon, Ursula.** *Nurk: The Strange, Surprising Adventures of a (Somewhat) Brave Shrew.* **Harcourt, 2008. 131 p.**
Gr. K–4. Nurk is the grandson of the legendary warrior shrew Surka. His grandmother hasn't been seen for several seasons, but her exploits are well known. Nurk dreams about going on an adventure. A letter arrives that changes his life. He makes a "Snailboat" and goes downstream. He finds a dragonfly princess whose brother has been captured by the dreaded Grizzlemole. Nurk sets out to free the dragonfly.

10-Minute Selection: Read chapter 9. Nurk leaves his Snailboat and ventures on foot to find the prince. He hears a scary noise. "It was a swallowing, smacking, gnarfing, gnorbling kind of noise." He bravely enters a metal drainpipe and finds, to his relief, that the cause of the sound is a tiny caterpillar. "Every bite it took, the sound was carried into the metal drainpipe, where it echoed and rang down the length, coming out vastly magnified." Moments after Nurk lets out a sigh, he feels a drop of slime on his back and finds himself surrounded by several monstrous caterpillars. Once he cleverly works his way out of that situation, Nurk confronts another problem: a wall of tall mushrooms that dump sneeze-inducing spores. "The spores were worse than pepper, worse than hay fever, worse than anything. He had never sneezed so hard in his life." Once again Nurk uses his wits to overcome a problem. The chapter ends with him entering the Grizzlemole's tunnel.

**Voake, Steve.** *Daisy Dawson Is On Her Way!* **Candlewick, 2008. 98 p.**
Gr. K–3. Daisy Dawson dawdles on her way to school every day and is constantly late. Today, she stops to help a butterfly out of a spider's web. As it flies away, the butterfly brushes Daisy's cheek. "Her cheeks began to tingle as though something was sparkling beneath her skin." Daisy learns that she can now understand animals and speak to them. She meets Boom, a dog, who loves Daisy's ham sandwiches. Daisy also converses with the two pet gerbils, a lost ant, a snobbish cat named Trixie McDixie, a horse named Meadowsweet, and Cyril the squirrel. The animals help Daisy rescue Boom from the new dogcatcher.

10-Minute Selection: Read the hilarious chapter 3, "Ant Music." Daisy hears a tiny voice singing, "Dubbedy dum-dum, dee dubbedy, dubbedy dum-dum, dee dubbedy." It's an ant. The ant panics when he sees Daisy. "Don't step on me with those big shoes!" Daisy convinces him that she's friendly. She correctly guesses the name of his song—"Dubbedy Dum-Dum." The ant has lost his patrol and wants to return home. Daisy helps him but is stopped by her principal on her way out. She tells the ant to shut up, and the principal assumes she's talking to him. The ant's dialogue is in a small font size and begs to be read in a high voice.

**Weaver, Will.** *Memory Boy.* **HarperCollins, 2001. 152 p.**
Gr. 4–12. "Washington State has been rocked by major volcanic eruptions. . . . Mount Rainier exploded with cataclysmic force." Volcanic ash has ruined crops, and folks are fleeing urban areas because of increasing looting and violence. Fifteen-year-old Miles creates a vehicle with six bicycle wheels and a sail and calls it the Ali Princess. He and his family leave the Twin Cities and head for their cabin in northern Minnesota. When they arrive, they find squatters on their land, including a heavily armed ex-con. Miles convinces his family to continue north to locate a cabin where an elderly man he met once lived.

10-Minute Selection: Read the above annotation to your audience, minus the last two sentences. Then read the second half of chapter 5, "Adios." Begin with the sentence, "I woke to the sound of panting," and read to the chapter's end. After traveling all day, Miles' family hide the Ali Princess and walk into a town to eat. The locals make them feel very unwelcome, even charging them almost a hundred dollars for a McDonald's breakfast. Read the first few pages of chapter 7, "Broad Daylight." Miles is worried about the campsite they chose. He has everyone move away from the highway. At bedtime, Miles walks near their first campsite. He hears two male voices. "Looks like they may have stopped here, but they musta kept going. . . . They had money on them, I know it." They move on, but Miles stays awake for a long time. Finish with the sentence, "I kept imagining I could smell cigarette smoke."

**Weeks, Sarah.** *Oggie Cooder.* **Scholastic, 2008. 172 p.**
Gr. 3–5. Oggie has a unique talent. He carves pieces of cheese into the shape of states with his teeth. Oggie is also somewhat of an oddball to his classmates. However, once a famous television talent show gets wind of Oggie, his popularity soars. Soon, everyone wants to be his friend. Unfortunately, Oggie's neighbor Donnica decides to become his manager and takes control of his life.

10-Minute Selection: Before reading, explain to your students that the word *charving* is a word created by combining the words *chewing* and *carving*. Read the humorous opening chapter. We get to learn a little of Oggie's peculiarities. He's bitter because he didn't win a contest naming a new type of cinnamon-raisin bagel. He thinks the winning name, "Sunshine," is a poor choice. Move on to chapter 4. Oggie and his classmates are taking a spelling test. They are to use the word in a sentence and then pass their papers to their neighbors to grade. Continue reading the short chapter 5. A girl named America tries to read Oggie's handwriting. "'Someone is a ridiculous man funny bongo,' said America." When Oggie reads aloud what he wrote—"Sunshine is a ridiculous name for a bagel"— the kids respond with, "That doesn't make any more sense than the bongo one." It turns out that all of Oggie's spelling sentences angrily refer to the winning bagel named Sunshine.

**Weeks, Sarah. *So. B. It.* HarperCollins, 2004. 243 p.**
Gr. 4–8. Twelve-year-old Heidi hops on a bus by herself and travels from Nevada to New York to learn about her mysterious past. As an infant, she had appeared out of nowhere on Bernadette's doorstep with her mother, a mentally disabled woman whose vocabulary is limited to twenty-three words. Heidi knows the journey will change her life. "But the truth was, I would not be back at all. Not as the same person I was that day, anyway." This powerful, multidimensional, realistic story contains a touch of magic and will move all listeners.

10-Minute Selection: Read the last third of chapter 3, "Hello." Begin with the sentence, "We don't know exactly when my birthday is because I don't have a birth certificate, and Mama didn't know when her own birthday was," and continue to the end of the chapter. Heidi tells how she and her mother wound up living with Bernadette. The passage ends with Heidi believing that's when her good luck kicked in. Continue reading chapter 8, "More." Heidi uses her good luck to win enough money for the bus trip. She also plots how to buy the ticket and board the bus despite the fact that she's too young to do either by herself.

**Werlin, Nancy. *The Rules of Survival.* Dial, 2006. 260 p.**
Gr. 8–12. Matt tries to protect his two younger sisters from their abusive mother, Nikki, in this dark novel. Nikki is prone to fits of rage; she's physically and emotionally abusive. As Matt puts it, "Our mother, Nicole Marie Walsh, was a true wacko." The kids befriend a man named Murdoch, half hoping he will save them from their situation. Murdoch dates Nikki for a little while until he learns about her dark side. In doing so, he, along with the kids, is in real danger from Nikki's obsessive hate.

10-Minute Selection: Read chapter 12, "Fun, Fun, Fun." Nikki makes the kids participate "in a frantic round of enforced family fun." She drives the kids to a pancake house and then a carnival. Your listeners will get a taste of Nikki's evil on the ride home. She drives the Jeep on the wrong side of the road and says, "I go to a lot of trouble for you kids. . . . I love you to death, but this is one of those times when I think I'm not appreciated. . . . Tell me you love me best. . . . Convince me, Matthew." Matthew screams that she's the best mother in the world moments before Nikki swerves back into her lane, narrowly missing another car. "Oh, now *that* was fun. Wasn't that fun, guys? Sort of like a roller coaster."

**Winerip, Michael.** *Adam Canfield of the Slash.* **Candlewick, 2005. 326 p.**
Gr. 5–7. Adam and Jennifer are coeditors of the school newspaper, the *Slash*. They start to uncover a big story that involves both city and school scandals. When the kids write a tribute to Eddie the janitor, Mrs. Marris insists they remove the following lines: "His newest project is building Mrs. Marris a set of cabinets for an electronic system she's having installed in the principal's office. He's also remodeling her bathroom." When the kids balk, Mrs. Marris reacts by shouting, "I said take it out. I mean take it out. Am I speaking a foreign language? Take it out, take it out, take it out." The kids investigate and find that Mrs. Marris is diverting school gift funds for her personal use. This is the first book in a series.

10-Minute Selection: Read a section of chapter 5, "High-Pressure Smiling," starting with the sentence, "The press release said the contest was being held along the west strollway, in the opening by the Gap," through to the end of the chapter. Young reporter Phoebe covers a smiling contest held by local dentists. The child who smiles the longest wins the contest. Phoebe can't believe her eyes when she witnesses the contestants gobbling candy and soda during their breaks to get enough energy to keep smiling.

**Winthrop, Elizabeth.** *The Red-Hot Rattoons.* **Holt, 2003. 212 p.**
Gr. 4–5. Five young rats find themselves orphans when their musical parents are killed. The five—Benny, Fletcher, Ella, Woody and Monk—become a dance team with help from Uncle Switch. The Rattoons, as they now call themselves, head for the city to seek their fame but run into trouble from both humans and other rats.

10-Minute Selection: Read most of chapter 13, "The Performance," beginning with the sentence, "The day seemed to last forever." The Rattoons see a group of humans gathered around "a person in white robes with a painted white face." The Rattoons fall in behind the mime and catch the attention of the human crowd. The chapter ends with people realizing that what they thought were mice are really rats. Continue reading chapter 14, "Arrested." The humans flee in a stampede at the sight of the rats. The Rattoons make their way to a park only to be arrested by the 117th Battalion of the Designated Foragers, a rat army. "Because of the pandemonium you caused this afternoon in front of the museum, the humans will raise a hue and cry. . . . By your actions, you have endangered the life of every rat who works aboveground."

**Wolfson, Jill.** *Home, and Other Big, Fat Lies.* **Holt, 2006. 281 p.**
Gr. 4–8. Most of the logging families of Forest Glen, California, are out of work and depressed. Many families take in foster children for the money. Enter high-wired Whitney, aka Termite. She's been shuffled from one urban foster home to another. Now, she's in the country and starting a new school. She falls in love

with the forest and joins an ecology club in school. Unfortunately, *ecology* is not a popular term with most of the locals. Readers will have fun keeping up with Termite's first-person narrative. "It blasted out of me, a full-blown laughing attack, which is my wacky-monkey, cackling-chicken, mad-scientist, sputtering-car-starting, snorting-through-the nose, mouth-wide-open-cawing-crow laughs all rolled into one." She hangs out with several other foster children. When the local economy improves, the children are worried their families won't want them anymore. Whitney is also a character in the author's novel *What I Call Life*.

10-Minute Selection: Read chapter 2. Termite meets her new foster family. She gets wound up and throws up "a supersize bag's worth of sunflower seeds all over my open-toe sandals." Skip ahead and read Termite's funny handwritten "Science Fair Project Journal Entry #1," at the end of chapter 19. She experiments to see if banana slugs prefer bad breath or "a fresh, pepperminty scent."

**Wooding, Chris.** *Poison.* **Orchard, 2003. 273 p.**
Gr. 5–10. "Once upon a time there was a young lady who lived in a marsh, and her name was Poison." The headstrong sixteen-year-old chose her own name at her "nameday" to spite her stepmother, who once said, "You're poison to this family, poison!" Poison leaves home to retrieve her two-year-old sister, Azalea, who was stolen by the Scarecrow on behalf of the Phaerie Lord. She meets many formidable enemies and a few allies to help her on her quest. There are a handful of hard names to pronounce, but the rich characterizations, the nonstop action, and the plot twists—particularly on the very last page—make the efforts more than worthwhile.

10-Minute Selection: Read the chapter titled "The House of the Bone Witch." To get to the Realm of Phaerie to retrieve her sister, Poison must first go to the passing-place that is inhabited by Maeb, the Bone Witch. "She is blind and deaf, but do not be fooled. She can smell you. And she has two hounds, two hounds that can tear you limb to limb if they get hold of you." Poison sneaks in Maeb's house and prowls around, finding a cauldron and things—such as the balcony railing and chandelier—made from bones. The chapter ends when Poison hears a creak on the stairs, "and a thin, cracked voice floated through the house. 'I can smell you, my dear! I'll have your bones!' The Bone Witch was awake."

**Woodson, Jacqueline.** *Feathers.* **Putnam, 2007. 118 p.**
Gr. 5–9. Sixth-grader Frannie is pondering the meaning of Emily Dickinson's poem that contains the lines, "Hope is the thing with feathers / That perches in the soul." She's also observing the arrival of the only white boy in her school, a bully's attitude toward the new kid, her mother's pregnancy, her best friend's faith, and her brother's deafness.

10-Minute Selection: Read the first chapter, which describes Frannie's thoughts on the day the new boy arrived at school. "His coming into our classroom that morning was the only new thing. Everything else was the same way it'd always been." She observes Trevor's hostile reaction to the newcomer. The chapter ends with, "As we walked down the hall, I stared at Trevor's back, wondering how long the new boy would have to wait before he got his head slapped." Continue reading the short chapter 13, where Frannie is walking with her deaf brother, Sean. Two girls approach Sean and start flirting with him. They are surprised to learn he is deaf and make sarcastic remarks. We see his frustration when the one girl states, "Dang . . . all that fineness wasted."

**Woodson, Jacqueline. *Hush*. Putnam, 2002. 180 p.**
Gr. 5–10. Towiah gets a new name—Evie—when her family goes into a witness-protection program. Her father testified against fellow police officers in the fatal shooting of an African American boy, and the family started receiving death threats. The move has negatively affected the entire family. Evie's father is depressed and suicidal, her mother has joined a new religion, and her sister is looking for a way out of their current situation. Evie slowly makes friends in her new world and tries out for the school's track team.

10-Minute Selection: Read most of chapter 4, beginning with the sentence, "Things fall apart," and continue to the end of the chapter. Evie remembers the details of the shooting and is shocked to learn that the fifteen-year-old African American boy was "killed by two white cops who were close to our family." Her father is torn because he knows the boy was shot standing with his arms in the air, contrary to the official report that he was going for a gun.

**Woodson, Jacqueline. *Miracle's Boys*. Putnam, 2000. 131 p.**
Gr. 6–10. Three brothers try to survive after, first, the death of their father and then, years later, the death of their mother. The middle boy, Charlie, has come home after years in a juvenile-detention center. He blames the youngest brother, Lafayette, for their mother's death. Lafayette has renamed his brother Newcharlie, wishing he could get a glimpse at the older, kinder version of the brother he once knew.

10-Minute Selection: Before reading this selection, inform your audience that three brothers are living together after the death of their mother, Milagro, whose name means "miracle" in Spanish. Read the opening chapter. Charlie is hanging out with his tough friend Aaron. The two make harsh remarks to Lafayette while they debate which ethnic gangs are the "baddest." We learn about the two versions of Charlie—before he went to the Rahway Home for Boys and after he was released. Charlie tells the story of an inmate who made a weapon out of a shoehorn. The two boys leave the apartment with the following cutting remark aimed at Lafayette: "Later, Milagro killer."

**Yep, Laurence.** *The Earth Dragon Awakes: The San Francisco Earthquake of 1906.* **HarperCollins, 2006. 117 p.**
Gr. 3–6. Chin and his father, Ah Sing, work for the Travis family. They are in their Chinatown tenement when the 1906 San Francisco earthquake strikes. The two work hard to survive the aftershocks and the subsequent fire dangers. In another section of the city, young Henry Travis and his family help their neighbors until fires drive them from their home. The two parties eventually reunite among the city ruins.

10-Minute Selection: Read the four consecutive entries starting with "10:30 a.m. Wednesday, April 18, 1906, the Travises' house, Sacramento Street area" through "3:00 p.m. Wednesday, April 18, 1906, from the Travises' house to northern San Francisco." The first short entry shows the stream of people passing by the Travis family and fleeing the fires. The second entry shows Chin and Ah Sing making their way to the waterfront. This entry ends with the line, "Chin says a prayer for Henry." The pagelong third entry describes three fires swallowing everything in their paths. The last entry follows the Travis family again. They join the crowd of people. "Suddenly the street explodes." The gas mains have broken. The chapter ends with, "Henry hopes Chin has gotten away in time."

**Ylvisaker, Anne.** *Little Klein.* **Candlewick, 2007. 186 p.**
Gr. 4–6. Little Klein is not only the youngest of the four Klein brothers but he is also the smallest in stature. Sometimes, he is overly protected by his mother. Other times, he is ignored. He finally gets his message of wanting a dog through when he brings home a rambunctious stray they name LeRoy. Trouble occurs when the three older boys go over a waterfall on their homemade raft shortly before a tornado hits the area.

10-Minute Selection: Read the chapter titled "Castle." With the house empty, Little Klein lets LeRoy into the house for the first time. He tries to get LeRoy to learn how to eat on a chair at the kitchen table and also leads him to the bathroom. "The bathroom offered a bowl of fragrant water—an indoor pond!" LeRoy is spoiled from his visit. His "doghouse felt unbearably small and cramped and devoid of aroma." Continue reading the next chapter, "Recipe for Sleep." Little Klein has nightmares and begs his mother to allow LeRoy to sleep with him. She resists. They fall into a routine of his mother reading recipes to Little Klein until he falls asleep. She finally grows tired of this method and tells Little Klein to send for his dog.

**Yolen, Jane, and Robert J. Harris.** *Girl in a Cage.* **Philomel, 2002. 230 p.**
Gr. 5–12. Eleven-year-old Marjorie is the daughter of the new Scottish king, Robert the Bruce. English forces, led by Edward Longshanks, king of England, capture

Marjorie. Marjorie is forced to spend nearly three weeks locked in a cage and put on display, where she is jeered by English peasants. Even though she becomes filthy and thin, she is determined to present herself as a true princess. This is the second book in the authors' Stuart Quartet.

10-Minute Selection: Read the very short first chapter, which opens with the sentence, "Dear Lord, if it is not too much to ask, could you please send less wind and fewer turnips?" Marjorie has little shelter from the weather in her cage. And "the good folk of Lanercost" throw the turnips at her. Continue reading the next two chapters. Marjorie recounts her trip to Lanercost. "The soldiers who surrounded me seemed embarrassed. So many of them needed to guard one small girl." She is shocked when she realizes that, instead of being held captive in the priory, she is to be displayed in "a cage of latticed timber and iron." If there is time, read one of the confrontations between Marjorie and Longshanks that reveal the girl's determination to not give in to her cruel captor. In chapter 22, begin with the sentence, "If I am to be silent in Longshanks' presence, my body must be mute as well." Read up to the line, "If I can truly make it so, I will beat him forever."

**Zusak, Markus.** *The Book Thief.* **Knopf, 2006. 552 p.**
Gr. 8–12. The place and time is Molching, Germany, immediately before and during World War II. The book thief is a young girl named Liesel. She and her new foster parents hide Max, a Jew, in their basement. She runs around with her neighbor Rudy, and the two steal items, such as food from farms. Liesel's favorite things to steal, however, are books. Her papa teaches her how to read, and she eventually writes an autobiography, *The Book Thief.* Her story is found and narrated by none other than Death. There are many German phrases to read and some strong language. But anyone who reads or listens to this story will likely be moved enough to remember it for a lifetime.

10-Minute Selection: There are several chapters that make excellent stand-alone reads, such as "Tricksters," "The Visitor," and "The Collector." One passage that works especially well in this regard is the chapter titled "The Whistler and the Shoes." Rudy has had a string of bad luck, culminating in being forced to do drop-down drills in manure for a mean Hitler Youth leader. Liesel realizes that Rudy needs a win. "They had to steal something." They decide to steal from the mayor's house. After all, the mayor and his wife had fired Liesel's mother. Liesel decides to climb through a window and steal a book titled *The Whistler.* As the two run home, Rudy calls her a book thief. "It was the first time Liesel had been branded with her title, and she couldn't hide the fact that she liked it very much… she had stolen books previously, but in late October 1941, it became official. That night, Liesel Meminger truly became the book thief."

# Books by Subject

## Animals

Armstrong, Alan. *Whittington.*
Auch, Mary Jane. *I Was a Third Grade Spy.*
Avi. *Ereth's Birthday.*
Byars, Betsy. *Me Tarzan.*
Delaney, Michael. *Birdbrain Amos.*
Denslow, Sharon Phillips. *Georgie Lee.*
DiCamillo, Kate. *Because of Winn-Dixie.*
———. *The Tale of Despereaux.*
Dunrea, Olivier. *Hanne's Quest.*
Elliott, David. *Evangeline Mudd and the Golden-Haired Apes of the Ikkinasti Jungle.*
Hale, Bruce. *The Possum Always Rings Twice.*
Hunter, Erin. *Warriors: Into the Wild.*
Jonell, Lynne. *Emmy and the Incredible Shrinking Rat.*
King-Smith, Dick. *Lady Lollipop.*
Maguire, Gregory. *Leaping Beauty and Other Animal Fairy Tales.*
Michael, Livi. *City of Dogs.*
Naylor, Phyllis Reynolds. *Polo's Mother.*
O'Connor, Barbara. *How to Steal a Dog.*
Pratchett, Terry. *The Amazing Maurice and His Educated Rodents.*
Ryan, Pam Muñoz. *Paint the Wind.*
Springer, Nancy, ed. *Ribbiting Tales: Original Stories about Frogs.*
Staples, Suzanne Fisher. *The Green Dog.*
Vernon, Ursula. *Nurk: The Strange, Surprising Adventures of a (Somewhat) Brave Shrew.*

Voake, Steve. *Daisy Dawson Is On Her Way!*
Winthrop, Elizabeth. *The Red-Hot Rattoons.*
Ylvisaker, Anne. *Little Klein.*


## Ecology

Elliott, David. *Evangeline Mudd and the Golden-Haired Apes of the Ikkinasti Jungle.*
Hiaasen, Carl. *Flush.*
————. *Hoot.*
Hobbs, Will. *Wild Man Island.*
Van Draanen, Wendelin. *Sammy Keyes and the Wild Things.*
Wolfson, Jill. *Home, and Other Big, Fat Lies.*


## Family

Archer, Lily. *The Poison Apples.*
Birdsall, Jeanne. *The Penderwicks: A Summer Tale of Four Sisters, Two Rabbits, and a Very Interesting Boy.*
Blume, Judy. *Soupy Saturdays with the Pain and the Great One.*
Bowler, Tim. *Storm Catchers.*
Byars, Betsy. *Keeper of the Doves.*
Cabot, Meg. *Jinx.*
Cameron, Ann. *Gloria's Way.*
Creech, Sharon. *Granny Torrelli Makes Soup.*
————. *Heartbeat.*
————. *The Wanderer.*
Cutler, Jane. *Leap, Frog.*
Denslow, Sharon Phillips. *Georgie Lee.*
Dowd, Siobhan. *The London Eye Mystery.*
Dowell, Frances O'Roark. *Dovey Coe.*
Fine, Anne. *The Jamie and Angus Stories.*
Flake, Sharon B. *Begging for Change.*
Giff, Patricia Reilly. *Willow Run.*
Graff, Nancy Price. *Taking Wing.*
Haddix, Margaret Peterson. *Say What?*
Johnson, Angela. *Bird.*
Look, Lenore. *Alvin Ho: Allergic to Girls, School, and Other Scary Things.*
————. *Ruby Lu, Empress of Everything.*

Lord, Cynthia. *Rules.*
McDonald, Megan. *Judy Moody.*
————. *Stink and the Incredible Super-Galactic Jawbreaker.*
Morpurgo, Michael. *Private Peaceful.*
O'Connor, Barbara. *How to Steal a Dog.*
Paterson, Katherine. *The Same Stuff as Stars.*
Pearsall, Shelley. *All Shook Up.*
Resau, Laura. *Red Glass.*
Roberts, Diane. *Made You Look.*
Ryan, Pam Muñoz. *Becoming Naomi León.*
————. *Esperanza Rising.*
Schmidt, Gary D. *The Wednesday Wars.*
Staples, Suzanne Fisher. *The Green Dog.*
Weaver, Will. *Memory Boy.*
Weeks, Sarah. *So. B. It.*
Werlin, Nancy. *The Rules of Survival.*
Wolfson, Jill. *Home, and Other Big, Fat Lies.*
Woodson, Jacqueline. *Feathers.*
————. *Hush.*
————. *Miracle's Boys.*

## Fantasy and Science Fiction

Armstrong, Alan. *Whittington.*
Auch, Mary Jane. *I Was a Third Grade Spy.*
Avi. *Ereth's Birthday.*
Bruchac, Joseph. *The Dark Pond.*
Buckley, Michael. *The Sisters Grimm, Book One: The Fairy Tale Detectives.*
Colfer, Eoin. *Artemis Fowl.*
————. *The Supernaturalist.*
Collins, Ross. *Medusa Jones.*
Coombs, Kate. *The Runaway Princess.*
Craig, Joe. *Jimmy Coates: Assassin?*
Delaney, Joseph. *The Last Apprentice: Revenge of the Witch.*
Delaney, Michael. *Birdbrain Amos.*
DiCamillo, Kate. *The Miraculous Journey of Edward Tulane.*
————. *The Tale of Despereaux.*
Dunrea, Olivier. *Hanne's Quest.*
DuPrau, Jeanne. *The City of Ember.*
Dyer, Heather. *Ibby's Magic Weekend.*

Elliott, David. *Evangeline Mudd and the Golden-Haired Apes of the Ikkinasti Jungle.*

Funke, Cornelia. *Igraine the Brave.*

———. *Inkheart.*

Gaiman, Neil. *Coraline.*

Gardner, Lyn. *Into the Woods.*

Grant, Michael. *Gone.*

Haddix, Margaret Peterson. *Found.*

Hale, Bruce. *The Possum Always Rings Twice.*

Hale, Shannon. *The Goose Girl.*

———. *Princess Academy.*

Hautman, Peter. *Rash.*

Higgins, F. E. *The Black Book of Secrets.*

Hunter, Erin. *Warriors: Into the Wild.*

Jenkins, Emily. *Toys Go Out.*

Jonell, Lynne. *Emmy and the Incredible Shrinking Rat.*

King-Smith, Dick. *Lady Lollipop.*

Landy, Derek. *Skulduggery Pleasant.*

Lorey, Dean. *Nightmare Academy.*

Lowry, Lois. *Gathering Blue.*

Maguire, Gregory. *Leaping Beauty and Other Animal Fairy Tales.*

———. *Three Rotten Eggs.*

Marcantonio, Patricia Santos. *Red Ridin' in the Hood and Other Cuentos.*

Michael, Livi. *City of Dogs.*

Morris, Gerald. *The Lioness and Her Knight.*

Naylor, Phyllis Reynolds. *Polo's Mother.*

Park, Linda Sue. *Archer's Quest.*

Petty, J. T. *Clemency Pogue: Fairy Killer.*

Pfeffer, Susan. *Life as We Knew It.*

Pratchett, Terry. *The Amazing Maurice and His Educated Rodents.*

———. *The Wee Free Men: A Story of Discworld.*

Pullman, Philip. *I Was a Rat!*

———. *The Scarecrow and His Servant.*

Riordan, Rick. *The Lightning Thief.*

Sage, Angie. *My Haunted House.*

Scieszka, Jon. *See You Later, Gladiator.*

Shalant, Phyllis. *The Great Cape Rescue.*

Shusterman, Neal. *Dread Locks.*

———. *Unwind.*

Soto, Gary. *Afterlife.*

Springer, Nancy, ed. *Ribbiting Tales: Original Stories about Frogs.*
Vernon, Ursula. *Nurk: The Strange, Surprising Adventures of a (Somewhat) Brave Shrew.*
Voake, Steve. *Daisy Dawson Is On Her Way!*
Winthrop, Elizabeth. *The Red-Hot Rattoons.*
Wooding, Chris. *Poison.*

## Friendship

Archer, Lily. *The Poison Apples.*
Barrows, Annie. *Ivy and Bean and the Ghost That Had to Go.*
Bauer, Marion Dane. *The Double-Digit Club.*
Birdsall, Jeanne. *The Penderwicks: A Summer Tale of Four Sisters, Two Rabbits, and a Very Interesting Boy.*
Bowe, Julie. *My Last Best Friend.*
Cameron, Ann. *Gloria's Way.*
Creech, Sharon. *Granny Torrelli Makes Soup.*
————. *Heartbeat.*
Cummings, Priscilla. *Red Kayak.*
Cutler, Jane. *Leap, Frog.*
Draper, Sharon M. *Double Dutch.*
Flake, Sharon B. *Begging for Change.*
Glatshteyn, Yankev. *Emil and Karl.*
Kerrin, Jessica Scott. *Martin Bridge: Ready for Takeoff!*
Look, Lenore. *Alvin Ho: Allergic to Girls, School, and Other Scary Things.*
Soto, Gary. *Worlds Apart: Traveling with Fernie and Me.*
Weeks, Sarah. *Oggie Cooder.*

## Ghost Stories/Horror

Bowler, Tim. *Storm Catchers.*
Bruchac, Joseph. *The Dark Pond.*
Delaney, Joseph. *The Last Apprentice: Revenge of the Witch.*
Gaiman, Neil. *Coraline.*
Landy, Derek. *Skulduggery Pleasant.*
Sage, Angie. *My Haunted House.*
Soto, Gary. *Afterlife.*

## Historical Fiction

Anderson, Laurie Halse. *Fever 1793.*
Avi. *The Secret School.*
————. *The Traitor's Gate.*
Birney, Betty G. *The Seven Wonders of Sassafras Springs.*
Byars, Betsy. *Keeper of the Doves.*
Curtis, Christopher Paul. *Elijah of Buxton.*
Cushman, Karen. *Matilda Bone.*
————. *Rodzina.*
Dowell, Frances O'Roark. *Dovey Coe.*
Erdrich, Louise. *The Game of Silence.*
Giff, Patricia Reilly. *Willow Run.*
Glatshteyn, Yankev. *Emil and Karl.*
Graff, Nancy Price. *Taking Wing.*
Hill, Kirkpatrick. *The Year of Miss Agnes.*
Larson, Kirby. *Hattie Big Sky.*
McCaughrean, Geraldine. *Cyrano.*
————. *The Kite Rider.*
Miller, Sarah. *Miss Spitfire: Reaching Helen Keller.*
Morpurgo, Michael. *Private Peaceful.*
Myers, Walter Dean. *Harlem Summer.*
————. *Sunrise over Fallujah.*
Peck, Richard. *On the Wings of Heroes.*
————. *The Teacher's Funeral: A Comedy in Three Parts.*
Ryan, Pam Muñoz. *Esperanza Rising.*
Salisbury, Graham. *Eyes of the Emperor.*
Schmidt, Gary D. *The Wednesday Wars.*
Smith, D. James. *The Boys of San Joaquin.*
Yep, Laurence. *The Earth Dragon Awakes: The San Francisco Earthquake of 1906.*
Yolen, Jane, and Robert J. Harris. *Girl in a Cage.*
Zusak, Markus. *The Book Thief.*

## Humor

Avi. *Ereth's Birthday.*
Barrows, Annie. *Ivy and Bean and the Ghost That Had to Go.*
Blume, Judy. *Soupy Saturdays with the Pain and the Great One.*
Byars, Betsy. *Me Tarzan.*
Byars, Betsy, Betsy Duffey, and Laurie Myers. *The SOS File.*

Clements, Andrew. *Jake Drake, Class Clown.*
————. *No Talking.*
Curtis, Christopher Paul. *Mr. Chickee's Funny Money.*
Cutler, Jane. *Leap, Frog.*
Delaney, Michael. *Birdbrain Amos.*
Elliott, David. *Evangeline Mudd and the Golden-Haired Apes of the Ikkinasti
    Jungle.*
Hale, Bruce. *The Possum Always Rings Twice.*
Horvath, Polly. *The Pepins and Their Problems.*
Jonell, Lynne. *Emmy and the Incredible Shrinking Rat.*
Korman, Gordon. *No More Dead Dogs.*
Look, Lenore. *Alvin Ho: Allergic to Girls, School, and Other Scary Things.*
Lowry, Lois. *Gooney Bird Greene.*
Maguire, Gregory. *Leaping Beauty and Other Animal Fairy Tales.*
McDonald, Megan. *Judy Moody.*
Mercado, Nancy E., ed. *Tripping Over the Lunch Lady and Other School Stories.*
Paulsen, Gary. *How Angel Peterson Got His Name and Other Outrageous Tales
    about Extreme Sports.*
Peck, Richard. *The Teacher's Funeral: A Comedy in Three Parts.*
Pennypacker, Sara. *The Talented Clementine.*
Rallison, Janette. *All's Fair in Love, War, and High School.*
Scieszka, Jon. *See You Later, Gladiator.*
Voake, Steve. *Daisy Dawson Is On Her Way!*
Weeks, Sarah. *Oggie Cooder.*

## Mystery

Abrams, Peter. *Down the Rabbit Hole.*
Avi. *The Traitor's Gate.*
Bauer, Joan. *Peeled.*
Bowler, Tim. *Storm Catchers.*
Broach, Elise. *Shakespeare's Secret.*
Bruchac, Joseph. *Bearwalker.*
Buckley, Michael. *The Sisters Grimm, Book One: The Fairy Tale Detectives.*
Dowd, Siobhan. *The London Eye Mystery.*
Dowell, Frances O'Roark. *Dovey Coe.*
DuPrau, Jeanne. *The City of Ember.*
Haddix, Margaret Peterson. *Found.*
Hale, Bruce. *The Possum Always Rings Twice.*
Hautman, Peter, and Mary Logue. *Snatched.*

Stewart, Trenton Lee. *The Mysterious Benedict Society.*
Van Draanen, Wendelin. *Sammy Keyes and the Wild Things.*


## Outdoor Survival

Bruchac, Joseph. *Bearwalker.*
Clements, Andrew. *A Week in the Woods.*
Fama, Elizabeth. *Overboard.*
Hobbs, Will. *Wild Man Island.*
Key, Watt. *Alabama Moon.*
Korman, Gordon. *Island: Book One; Shipwreck.*
Naylor, Phyllis Reynolds. *Roxie and the Hooligans.*
Paulsen, Gary. *Brian's Hunt.*
Philbrick, Rodman. *The Young Man and the Sea.*
Salisbury, Graham. *Night of the Howling Dogs.*
Shahan, Sherry. *Death Mountain.*
Smelcer, John. *The Trap.*
Smith, Roland. *Peak.*
Thomas, Jane Resh. *Blind Mountain.*
Weaver, Will. *Memory Boy.*


## People with Disabilities

Bauer, Marion Dane. *The Double-Digit Club.*
Bledsoe, Lucy Jane. *Hoop Girlz.*
Byars, Betsy. *Keeper of the Doves.*
Creech, Sharon. *Granny Torrelli Makes Soup.*
Dowd, Siobhan. *The London Eye Mystery.*
Dowell, Frances O'Roark. *Dovey Coe.*
Hill, Kirkpatrick. *The Year of Miss Agnes.*
Look, Lenore. *Ruby Lu, Empress of Everything.*
Lord, Cynthia. *Rules.*
Lowry, Lois. *Gathering Blue.*
Mackel, Kathy. *MadCat.*
Miller, Sarah. *Miss Spitfire: Reaching Helen Keller.*
Morpurgo, Michael. *Private Peaceful.*
Sachar, Louis. *Small Steps.*
Smith, D. James. *The Boys of San Joaquin.*
Woodson, Jacqueline. *Feathers.*

## Politics

Bauer, Joan. *Hope Was Here.*
———. *Peeled.*
Hale, Bruce. *The Possum Always Rings Twice.*
Naidoo, Beverley. *The Other Side of Truth.*
Rallison, Janette. *All's Fair in Love, War, and High School.*


## School

Archer, Lily. *The Poison Apples.*
Auch, Mary Jane. *I Was a Third Grade Spy.*
Avi. *The Secret School.*
Barrows, Annie. *Ivy and Bean and the Ghost That Had to Go.*
Bauer, Joan. *Peeled.*
Bruchac, Joseph. *Bearwalker.*
Byars, Betsy. *Me Tarzan.*
Byars, Betsy, Betsy Duffey, and Laurie Myers. *The SOS File.*
Cabot, Meg. *Jinx.*
Clements, Andrew. *Jake Drake, Class Clown.*
———. *No Talking.*
———. *A Week in the Woods.*
Dowell, Frances O'Roark. *Phineas L. MacGuire . . . Erupts! The First Experiment.*
Draper, Sharon M. *Double Dutch.*
Gantos, Jack. *Jack Adrift: Fourth Grade without a Clue.*
Grimes, Nikki. *Bronx Masquerade.*
Hale, Bruce. *The Possum Always Rings Twice.*
Hale, Shannon. *Princess Academy.*
Harkrader, L. D. *Airball: My Life in Briefs.*
Heneghan, James. *Payback.*
Hill, Kirkpatrick. *The Year of Miss Agnes.*
Korman, Gordon. *No More Dead Dogs.*
Look, Lenore. *Alvin Ho: Allergic to Girls, School, and Other Scary Things.*
———. *Ruby Lu, Empress of Everything.*
Lowry, Lois. *Gooney Bird Greene.*
Maguire, Gregory. *Three Rotten Eggs.*
Marsden, Carolyn. *Moon Runner.*
McDonald, Megan. *Judy Moody.*
Mercado, Nancy E., ed. *Tripping Over the Lunch Lady and Other School Stories.*
Morgenstern, Susie. *A Book of Coupons.*

Nagdo, Ann Whitehead. *Tarantula Power*.
Park, Linda Sue. *Project Mulberry*.
Pearsall, Shelley. *All Shook Up*.
Peck, Richard. *The Teacher's Funeral: A Comedy in Three Parts*.
Pennypacker, Sara. *The Talented Clementine*.
Rallison, Janette. *All's Fair in Love, War, and High School*.
Schmidt, Gary D. *The Wednesday Wars*.
Schwartz, Virginia Frances. *4 Kids in 5E and 1 Crazy Year*.
Shalant, Phyllis. *The Great Cape Rescue*.
Soto, Gary. *Worlds Apart: Traveling with Fernie and Me*.
Spinelli, Jerry. *Stargirl*.
Stewart, Trenton Lee. *The Mysterious Benedict Society*.
Winerip, Michael. *Adam Canfield of the Slash*.
Wolfson, Jill. *Home, and Other Big, Fat Lies*.
Woodson, Jacqueline. *Feathers*.

## Short Story Collections

Byars, Betsy, Betsy Duffey, and Laurie Myers. *The SOS File*.
Carter, Alden. *Love, Football, and Other Contact Sports*.
Gallo, Donald R., ed. *Destination Unexpected*.
———, ed. *First Crossing: Stories about Teen Immigrants*.
Maguire, Gregory. *Leaping Beauty and Other Animal Fairy Tales*.
Mercado, Nancy E., ed. *Tripping Over the Lunch Lady and Other School Stories*.
Paulsen, Gary. *How Angel Peterson Got His Name and Other Outrageous Tales about Extreme Sports*.
Peck, Richard. *Past Perfect, Present Tense: New and Collected Stories*.
Springer, Nancy, ed. *Ribbiting Tales: Original Stories about Frogs*.

## Sports

Bledsoe, Lucy Jane. *Hoop Girlz*.
Carter, Alden. *Love, Football, and Other Contact Sports*.
Creech, Sharon. *Heartbeat*.
Draper, Sharon M. *Double Dutch*.
Harkrader, L. D. *Airball: My Life in Briefs*.
Lupica, Mike. *Heat*.
Mackel, Kathy. *MadCat*.
Marsden, Carolyn. *Moon Runner*.

Murdock, Catherine Gilbert. *Dairy Queen.*
Napoli, Donna Jo, and Robert Furrow. *Sly the Sleuth and the Sports Mysteries.*
Paulsen, Gary. *How Angel Peterson Got His Name and Other Outrageous Tales about Extreme Sports.*
Ritter, John H. *The Boy Who Saved Baseball.*

## Stories Set in Other Countries

Bowler, Tim. *Storm Catchers.*
Craig, Joe. *Jimmy Coates: Assassin?*
Cushman, Karen. *Matilda Bone.*
Dowd, Siobhan. *The London Eye Mystery.*
Fama, Elizabeth. *Overboard.*
Glatshteyn, Yankev. *Emil and Karl.*
Heneghan, James. *Payback.*
Marcantonio, Patricia Santos. *Red Ridin' in the Hood and Other Cuentos.*
McCaughrean, Geraldine. *Cyrano.*
———. *The Kite Rider.*
Morgenstern, Susie. *A Book of Coupons.*
Morpurgo, Michael. *Private Peaceful.*
Morris, Gerald. *The Adventures of Sir Lancelot the Great.*
———. *The Lioness and Her Knight.*
Myers, Walter Dean. *Sunrise over Fallujah.*
Naidoo, Beverley. *The Other Side of Truth.*
Paulsen, Gary. *Brian's Hunt.*
Perkins, Mitali. *Rickshaw Girl.*
Resau, Laura. *Red Glass.*
Smith, Roland. *Peak.*
Zusak, Markus. *The Book Thief.*

# Grade-Level Recommendations

## Early Elementary (Grades K–2)

Auch, Mary Jane. *I Was a Third Grade Spy.*
Avi. *Ereth's Birthday.*
Barrows, Annie. *Ivy and Bean and the Ghost That Had to Go.*
Blume, Judy. *Soupy Saturdays with the Pain and the Great One.*
Byars, Betsy. *Me Tarzan.*
Byars, Betsy, Betsy Duffey, and Laurie Myers. *The SOS File.*
Cameron, Ann. *Gloria's Way.*
Clements, Andrew. *Jake Drake, Class Clown.*
Cutler, Jane. *Leap, Frog.*
Delaney, Michael. *Birdbrain Amos.*
Denslow, Sharon Phillips. *Georgie Lee.*
DiCamillo, Kate. *The Miraculous Journey of Edward Tulane.*
———. *The Tale of Despereaux.*
Dunrea, Olivier. *Hanne's Quest.*
Fine, Anne. *The Jamie and Angus Stories.*
Haddix, Margaret Peterson. *Say What?*
Hale, Bruce. *The Possum Always Rings Twice.*
Horvath, Polly. *The Pepins and Their Problems.*
Jenkins, Emily. *Toys Go Out.*
Kerrin, Jessica Scott. *Martin Bridge: Ready for Takeoff!*
King-Smith, Dick. *Lady Lollipop.*
Look, Lenore. *Alvin Ho: Allergic to Girls, School, and Other Scary Things.*
———. *Ruby Lu, Empress of Everything.*
Lowry, Lois. *Gooney Bird Greene.*

Maguire, Gregory. *Leaping Beauty and Other Animal Fairy Tales.*
McDonald, Megan. *Judy Moody.*
———. *Stink and the Incredible Super-Galactic Jawbreaker.*
Morris, Gerald. *The Adventures of Sir Lancelot the Great.*
Nagdo, Ann Whitehead. *Tarantula Power.*
Napoli, Donna Jo, and Robert Furrow. *Sly the Sleuth and the Sports Mysteries.*
Naylor, Phyllis Reynolds. *Polo's Mother.*
———. *Roxie and the Hooligans.*
Pennypacker, Sara. *The Talented Clementine.*
Sage, Angie. *My Haunted House.*
Scieszka, Jon. *See You Later, Gladiator.*
Vernon, Ursula. *Nurk: The Strange, Surprising Adventures of a (Somewhat) Brave Shrew.*
Voake, Steve. *Daisy Dawson Is On Her Way!*

## Upper Elementary (Grades 3–5)

Abrams, Peter. *Down the Rabbit Hole.*
Anderson, Laurie Halse. *Fever 1793.*
Armstrong, Alan. *Whittington.*
Auch, Mary Jane. *I Was a Third Grade Spy.*
Avi. *Ereth's Birthday.*
———. *The Secret School.*
———. *The Traitor's Gate.*
Barrows, Annie. *Ivy and Bean and the Ghost That Had to Go.*
Bauer, Marion Dane. *The Double-Digit Club.*
Birdsall, Jeanne. *The Penderwicks: A Summer Tale of Four Sisters, Two Rabbits, and a Very Interesting Boy.*
Birney, Betty G. *The Seven Wonders of Sassafras Springs.*
Bledsoe, Lucy Jane. *Hoop Girlz.*
Blume, Judy. *Soupy Saturdays with the Pain and the Great One.*
Bowe, Julie. *My Last Best Friend.*
Broach, Elise. *Shakespeare's Secret.*
Bruchac, Joseph. *Bearwalker.*
Buckley, Michael. *The Sisters Grimm, Book One: The Fairy Tale Detectives.*
Byars, Betsy. *Keeper of the Doves.*
———. *Me Tarzan.*
Byars, Betsy, Betsy Duffey, and Laurie Myers. *The SOS File.*
Cameron, Ann. *Gloria's Way.*
Clements, Andrew. *Jake Drake, Class Clown.*

————. *No Talking.*

————. *A Week in the Woods.*

Colfer, Eoin. *Artemis Fowl.*

————. *The Supernaturalist.*

Collins, Ross. *Medusa Jones.*

Coombs, Kate. *The Runaway Princess.*

Craig, Joe. *Jimmy Coates: Assassin?*

Creech, Sharon. *Granny Torrelli Makes Soup.*

————. *Heartbeat.*

————. *The Wanderer.*

Cummings, Priscilla. *Red Kayak.*

Curtis, Christopher Paul. *Elijah of Buxton.*

————. *Mr. Chickee's Funny Money.*

Cushman, Karen. *Matilda Bone.*

————. *Rodzina.*

Cutler, Jane. *Leap, Frog.*

Delaney, Joseph. *The Last Apprentice: Revenge of the Witch.*

Delaney, Michael. *Birdbrain Amos.*

DiCamillo, Kate. *Because of Winn-Dixie.*

————. *The Miraculous Journey of Edward Tulane.*

————. *The Tale of Despereaux.*

Dowell, Frances O'Roark. *Dovey Coe.*

————. *Phineas L. MacGuire . . . Erupts! The First Experiment.*

Draper, Sharon M. *Double Dutch.*

Dunrea, Olivier. *Hanne's Quest.*

DuPrau, Jeanne. *The City of Ember.*

Dyer, Heather. *Ibby's Magic Weekend.*

Elliott, David. *Evangeline Mudd and the Golden-Haired Apes of the Ikkinasti Jungle.*

Erdrich, Louise. *The Game of Silence.*

Fama, Elizabeth. *Overboard.*

Flake, Sharon B. *Begging for Change.*

Funke, Cornelia. *Igraine the Brave.*

————. *Inkheart.*

Gaiman, Neil. *Coraline.*

Gantos, Jack. *Jack Adrift: Fourth Grade without a Clue.*

Gardner, Lyn. *Into the Woods.*

Giff, Patricia Reilly. *Willow Run.*

Glatshteyn, Yankev. *Emil and Karl.*

Graff, Nancy Price. *Taking Wing.*

Haddix, Margaret Peterson. *Found.*

———. *Say What?*

Hale, Bruce. *The Possum Always Rings Twice.*

Hale, Shannon. *The Goose Girl.*

———. *Princess Academy.*

Harkrader, L. D. *Airball: My Life in Briefs.*

Hiaasen, Carl. *Flush.*

———. *Hoot.*

Higgins, F. E. *The Black Book of Secrets.*

Hill, Kirkpatrick. *The Year of Miss Agnes.*

Hobbs, Will. *Wild Man Island.*

Horvath, Polly. *The Pepins and Their Problems.*

Hunter, Erin. *Warriors: Into the Wild.*

Johnson, Angela. *Bird.*

Jonell, Lynne. *Emmy and the Incredible Shrinking Rat.*

Kerrin, Jessica Scott. *Martin Bridge: Ready for Takeoff!*

Key, Watt. *Alabama Moon.*

King-Smith, Dick. *Lady Lollipop.*

Korman, Gordon. *Island: Book One; Shipwreck.*

———. *No More Dead Dogs.*

Landy, Derek. *Skulduggery Pleasant.*

Look, Lenore. *Alvin Ho: Allergic to Girls, School, and Other Scary Things.*

———. *Ruby Lu, Empress of Everything.*

Lord, Cynthia. *Rules.*

Lorey, Dean. *Nightmare Academy.*

Lowry, Lois. *Gathering Blue.*

———. *Gooney Bird Greene.*

Lupica, Mike. *Heat.*

Mackel, Kathy. *MadCat.*

Maguire, Gregory. *Leaping Beauty and Other Animal Fairy Tales.*

———. *Three Rotten Eggs.*

Marcantonio, Patricia Santos. *Red Ridin' in the Hood and Other Cuentos.*

Marsden, Carolyn. *Moon Runner.*

McCaughrean, Geraldine. *The Kite Rider.*

McDonald, Megan. *Judy Moody.*

———. *Stink and the Incredible Super-Galactic Jawbreaker.*

Mercado, Nancy E., ed. *Tripping Over the Lunch Lady and Other School Stories.*

Michael, Livi. *City of Dogs.*

Miller, Sarah. *Miss Spitfire: Reaching Helen Keller.*

Morgenstern, Susie. *A Book of Coupons.*

Morris, Gerald. *The Adventures of Sir Lancelot the Great.*

———. *The Lioness and Her Knight.*

Nagdo, Ann Whitehead. *Tarantula Power.*
Naidoo, Beverley. *The Other Side of Truth.*
Napoli, Donna Jo, and Robert Furrow. *Sly the Sleuth and the Sports Mysteries.*
Naylor, Phyllis Reynolds. *Polo's Mother.*
————. *Roxie and the Hooligans.*
O'Connor, Barbara. *How to Steal a Dog.*
Park, Linda Sue. *Archer's Quest.*
————. *Project Mulberry.*
Paterson, Katherine. *The Same Stuff as Stars.*
Paulsen, Gary. *Brian's Hunt.*
————. *How Angel Peterson Got His Name and Other Outrageous Tales about Extreme Sports.*
Pearsall, Shelley. *All Shook Up.*
Peck, Richard. *On the Wings of Heroes.*
————. *Past Perfect, Present Tense: New and Collected Stories.*
————. *The Teacher's Funeral: A Comedy in Three Parts.*
Pennypacker, Sara. *The Talented Clementine.*
Perkins, Mitali. *Rickshaw Girl.*
Petty, J. T. *Clemency Pogue: Fairy Killer.*
Philbrick, Rodman. *The Young Man and the Sea.*
Pratchett, Terry. *The Amazing Maurice and His Educated Rodents.*
————. *The Wee Free Men: A Story of Discworld.*
Pullman, Philip. *I Was a Rat!*
————. *The Scarecrow and His Servant.*
Riordan, Rick. *The Lightning Thief.*
Ritter, John H. *The Boy Who Saved Baseball.*
Roberts, Diane. *Made You Look.*
Ryan, Pam Muñoz. *Becoming Naomi León.*
————. *Esperanza Rising.*
————. *Paint the Wind.*
Sachar, Louis. *Small Steps.*
Sage, Angie. *My Haunted House.*
Salisbury, Graham. *Night of the Howling Dogs.*
Schmidt, Gary D. *The Wednesday Wars.*
Schwartz, Virginia Frances. *4 Kids in 5E and 1 Crazy Year.*
Scieszka, Jon. *See You Later, Gladiator.*
Shahan, Sherry. *Death Mountain.*
Shalant, Phyllis. *The Great Cape Rescue.*
Smith, D. James. *The Boys of San Joaquin.*
Smith, Roland. *Peak.*
Soto, Gary. *Worlds Apart: Traveling with Fernie and Me.*

Springer, Nancy, ed. *Ribbiting Tales: Original Stories about Frogs.*
Staples, Suzanne Fisher. *The Green Dog.*
Stewart, Trenton Lee. *The Mysterious Benedict Society.*
Thomas, Jane Resh. *Blind Mountain.*
Van Draanen, Wendelin. *Sammy Keyes and the Wild Things.*
Vernon, Ursula. *Nurk: The Strange, Surprising Adventures of a (Somewhat) Brave Shrew.*
Voake, Steve. *Daisy Dawson Is On Her Way!*
Weaver, Will. *Memory Boy.*
Weeks, Sarah. *Oggie Cooder.*
————. *So. B. It.*
Winerip, Michael. *Adam Canfield of the Slash.*
Winthrop, Elizabeth. *The Red-Hot Rattoons.*
Wolfson, Jill. *Home, and Other Big, Fat Lies.*
Wooding, Chris. *Poison.*
Woodson, Jacqueline. *Feathers.*
————. *Hush.*
Yep, Laurence. *The Earth Dragon Awakes: The San Francisco Earthquake of 1906.*
Ylvisaker, Anne. *Little Klein.*
Yolen, Jane, and Robert J. Harris. *Girl in a Cage.*


## Middle School (Grades 6–8)

Abrams, Peter. *Down the Rabbit Hole.*
Anderson, Laurie Halse. *Fever 1793.*
Archer, Lily. *The Poison Apples.*
Armstrong, Alan. *Whittington.*
Avi. *Ereth's Birthday.*
————. *The Secret School.*
————. *The Traitor's Gate.*
Bauer, Joan. *Hope Was Here.*
————. *Peeled.*
Birdsall, Jeanne. *The Penderwicks: A Summer Tale of Four Sisters, Two Rabbits, and a Very Interesting Boy.*
Bowler, Tim. *Storm Catchers.*
Broach, Elise. *Shakespeare's Secret.*
Bruchac, Joseph. *Bearwalker.*
————. *The Dark Pond.*
Buckley, Michael. *The Sisters Grimm, Book One: The Fairy Tale Detectives.*
Byars, Betsy. *Keeper of the Doves.*

Cabot, Meg. *Jinx*.
Carter, Alden. *Love, Football, and Other Contact Sports*.
Clements, Andrew. *No Talking*.
———. *A Week in the Woods*.
Colfer, Eoin. *Artemis Fowl*.
———. *The Supernaturalist*.
Collins, Ross. *Medusa Jones*.
Coombs, Kate. *The Runaway Princess*.
Craig, Joe. *Jimmy Coates: Assassin?*
Creech, Sharon. *Granny Torrelli Makes Soup*.
———. *Heartbeat*.
———. *The Wanderer*.
Cummings, Priscilla. *Red Kayak*.
Curtis, Christopher Paul. *Elijah of Buxton*.
———. *Mr. Chickee's Funny Money*.
Cushman, Karen. *Matilda Bone*.
———. *Rodzina*.
Delaney, Joseph. *The Last Apprentice: Revenge of the Witch*.
Dowd, Siobhan. *The London Eye Mystery*.
Dowell, Frances O'Roark. *Dovey Coe*.
Draper, Sharon M. *Double Dutch*.
DuPrau, Jeanne. *Car Trouble*.
———. *The City of Ember*.
Dyer, Heather. *Ibby's Magic Weekend*.
Erdrich, Louise. *The Game of Silence*.
Fama, Elizabeth. *Overboard*.
Flake, Sharon B. *Begging for Change*.
Funke, Cornelia. *Igraine the Brave*.
———. *Inkheart*.
Gaiman, Neil. *Coraline*.
Gallo, Donald R., ed. *Destination Unexpected*.
———, ed. *First Crossing: Stories about Teen Immigrants*.
Gantos, Jack. *Jack Adrift: Fourth Grade without a Clue*.
Gardner, Lyn. *Into the Woods*.
Giff, Patricia Reilly. *Willow Run*.
Glatshteyn, Yankev. *Emil and Karl*.
Graff, Nancy Price. *Taking Wing*.
Grant, Michael. *Gone*.
Griffin, Adele. *My Almost Epic Summer*.
Grimes, Nikki. *Bronx Masquerade*.
Haddix, Margaret Peterson. *Found*.

Hale, Shannon. *The Goose Girl.*

———. *Princess Academy.*

Harkrader, L. D. *Airball: My Life in Briefs.*

Hautman, Peter. *Rash.*

Hautman, Peter, and Mary Logue. *Snatched.*

Heneghan, James. *Payback.*

Hiaasen, Carl. *Flush.*

———. *Hoot.*

Higgins, F. E. *The Black Book of Secrets.*

Hobbs, Will. *Wild Man Island.*

Horvath, Polly. *The Pepins and Their Problems.*

Hunter, Erin. *Warriors: Into the Wild.*

Johnson, Angela. *Bird.*

Key, Watt. *Alabama Moon.*

Korman, Gordon. *Island: Book One; Shipwreck.*

———. *No More Dead Dogs.*

Landy, Derek. *Skulduggery Pleasant.*

Larson, Kirby. *Hattie Big Sky.*

Lord, Cynthia. *Rules.*

Lorey, Dean. *Nightmare Academy.*

Lowry, Lois. *Gathering Blue.*

Lupica, Mike. *Heat.*

Mackel, Kathy. *MadCat.*

Maguire, Gregory. *Leaping Beauty and Other Animal Fairy Tales.*

———. *Three Rotten Eggs.*

Marcantonio, Patricia Santos. *Red Ridin' in the Hood and Other Cuentos.*

McCaughrean, Geraldine. *Cyrano.*

———. *The Kite Rider.*

Mercado, Nancy E., ed. *Tripping Over the Lunch Lady and Other School Stories.*

Michael, Livi. *City of Dogs.*

Miller, Sarah. *Miss Spitfire: Reaching Helen Keller.*

Morpurgo, Michael. *Private Peaceful.*

Morris, Gerald. *The Adventures of Sir Lancelot the Great.*

———. *The Lioness and Her Knight.*

Murdock, Catherine Gilbert. *Dairy Queen.*

Myers, Walter Dean. *Harlem Summer.*

———. *Sunrise over Fallujah.*

Naidoo, Beverley. *The Other Side of Truth.*

O'Connor, Barbara. *How to Steal a Dog.*

Park, Linda Sue. *Archer's Quest.*

Paterson, Katherine. *The Same Stuff as Stars.*

Paulsen, Gary. *Brian's Hunt.*

———. *How Angel Peterson Got His Name and Other Outrageous Tales about Extreme Sports.*

Pearsall, Shelley. *All Shook Up.*

Peck, Richard. *On the Wings of Heroes.*

———. *Past Perfect, Present Tense: New and Collected Stories.*

———. *The Teacher's Funeral: A Comedy in Three Parts.*

Petty, J. T. *Clemency Pogue: Fairy Killer.*

Pfeffer, Susan. *Life as We Knew It.*

Philbrick, Rodman. *The Young Man and the Sea.*

Pratchett, Terry. *The Amazing Maurice and His Educated Rodents.*

———. *The Wee Free Men: A Story of Discworld.*

Pullman, Philip. *I Was a Rat!*

———. *The Scarecrow and His Servant.*

Rallison, Janette. *All's Fair in Love, War, and High School.*

Riordan, Rick. *The Lightning Thief.*

Ritter, John H. *The Boy Who Saved Baseball.*

Roberts, Diane. *Made You Look.*

Ryan, Pam Muñoz. *Becoming Naomi León.*

———. *Esperanza Rising.*

———. *Paint the Wind.*

Sachar, Louis. *Small Steps.*

Salisbury, Graham. *Eyes of the Emperor.*

———. *Night of the Howling Dogs.*

Schmidt, Gary D. *The Wednesday Wars.*

Shahan, Sherry. *Death Mountain.*

Shusterman, Neal. *Dread Locks.*

———. *Unwind.*

Smelcer, John. *The Trap.*

Smith, D. James. *The Boys of San Joaquin.*

Smith, Roland. *Peak.*

Soto, Gary. *Afterlife.*

———. *Worlds Apart: Traveling with Fernie and Me.*

Spinelli, Jerry. *Stargirl.*

Stewart, Trenton Lee. *The Mysterious Benedict Society.*

Thomas, Jane Resh. *Blind Mountain.*

Van Draanen, Wendelin. *Sammy Keyes and the Wild Things.*

Weaver, Will. *Memory Boy.*

Weeks, Sarah. *So. B. It.*

Werlin, Nancy. *The Rules of Survival.*

Winerip, Michael. *Adam Canfield of the Slash.*

Wolfson, Jill. *Home, and Other Big, Fat Lies.*
Wooding, Chris. *Poison.*
Woodson, Jacqueline. *Feathers.*
———. *Hush.*
———. *Miracle's Boys.*
Yep, Laurence. *The Earth Dragon Awakes: The San Francisco Earthquake of 1906.*
Ylvisaker, Anne. *Little Klein.*
Yolen, Jane, and Robert J. Harris. *Girl in a Cage.*
Zusak, Markus. *The Book Thief.*


## High School (Grades 9–12)

Archer, Lily. *The Poison Apples.*
Bauer, Joan. *Hope Was Here.*
———. *Peeled.*
Bowler, Tim. *Storm Catchers.*
Bruchac, Joseph. *The Dark Pond.*
Cabot, Meg. *Jinx.*
Carter, Alden. *Love, Football, and Other Contact Sports.*
Colfer, Eoin. *Artemis Fowl.*
———. *The Supernaturalist.*
Cummings, Priscilla. *Red Kayak.*
Delaney, Joseph. *The Last Apprentice: Revenge of the Witch.*
Dowd, Siobhan. *The London Eye Mystery.*
DuPrau, Jeanne. *Car Trouble.*
———. *The City of Ember.*
Fama, Elizabeth. *Overboard.*
Flake, Sharon B. *Begging for Change.*
Funke, Cornelia. *Inkheart.*
Gaiman, Neil. *Coraline.*
Gallo, Donald R., ed. *Destination Unexpected.*
———, ed. *First Crossing: Stories about Teen Immigrants.*
Glatshteyn, Yankev. *Emil and Karl.*
Grant, Michael. *Gone.*
Grimes, Nikki. *Bronx Masquerade.*
Haddix, Margaret Peterson. *Found.*
Hautman, Peter. *Rash.*
Hautman, Peter, and Mary Logue. *Snatched.*
Heneghan, James. *Payback.*
Higgins, F. E. *The Black Book of Secrets.*

Hobbs, Will. *Wild Man Island.*
Johnson, Angela. *Bird.*
Landy, Derek. *Skulduggery Pleasant.*
Larson, Kirby. *Hattie Big Sky.*
Lupica, Mike. *Heat.*
Marcantonio, Patricia Santos. *Red Ridin' in the Hood and Other Cuentos.*
McCaughrean, Geraldine. *Cyrano.*
———. *The Kite Rider.*
Mercado, Nancy E., ed. *Tripping Over the Lunch Lady and Other School Stories.*
Miller, Sarah. *Miss Spitfire: Reaching Helen Keller.*
Morpurgo, Michael. *Private Peaceful.*
Morris, Gerald. *The Lioness and Her Knight.*
Murdock, Catherine Gilbert. *Dairy Queen.*
Myers, Walter Dean. *Harlem Summer.*
———. *Sunrise over Fallujah.*
Naidoo, Beverley. *The Other Side of Truth.*
Paulsen, Gary. *How Angel Peterson Got His Name and Other Outrageous Tales
    about Extreme Sports.*
Peck, Richard. *Past Perfect, Present Tense: New and Collected Stories.*
Pfeffer, Susan. *Life as We Knew It.*
Pratchett, Terry. *The Amazing Maurice and His Educated Rodents.*
———. *The Wee Free Men: A Story of Discworld.*
Rallison, Janette. *All's Fair in Love, War, and High School.*
Resau, Laura. *Red Glass.*
Riordan, Rick. *The Lightning Thief.*
Salisbury, Graham. *Eyes of the Emperor.*
Shusterman, Neal. *Dread Locks.*
———. *Unwind.*
Smelcer, John. *The Trap.*
Smith, Roland. *Peak.*
Soto, Gary. *Afterlife.*
Spinelli, Jerry. *Stargirl.*
Weaver, Will. *Memory Boy.*
Werlin, Nancy. *The Rules of Survival.*
Wooding, Chris. *Poison.*
Woodson, Jacqueline. *Feathers.*
———. *Hush.*
———. *Miracle's Boys.*
Yolen, Jane, and Robert J. Harris. *Girl in a Cage.*
Zusak, Markus. *The Book Thief.*

# You may also be interested in

***More Family Storytimes:*** This book features stories, fingerplays, songs, and movement activities to enhance the time families spend at the library. Brimming with all new material, it offers practical, creative, and active storytime programs that will captivate audiences of all ages.

***Something Musical Happened at the Library:*** Drawing on thousands of hours listening and programming, Reid selects the best of the best, presenting eight ready-to-use, comprehensive lesson plans to help you make music an everyday part of your programs.

***Cool Story Programs for the School-Age Crowd:*** What kid wouldn't love literary explorations of the stinky, creepy, and dirty? Throw in rats, witches, aliens, and underwear and it's irresistible. This proven, adaptable resource is for anyone who wants to help literature come alive for kids in grades K–4.

## Check out these and other great titles at www.alastore.ala.org!

***Book Links:*** The magazine that has been helping librarians, teachers, and parents connect children with high-quality books for more than fifteen years is where Reid began the "Reid-Aloud Alert" column that inspired *Reid's Read-Alouds*. Subscribe to *Book Links* at *www.ala.org/booklinks/.*